In Jutland with a Cycle.

Charles Edwardes

In Jutland with a Cycle.
Edwardes, Charles
British Library, Historical Print Editions
British Library
1897
x. 291 p. ; 8°.
10280.e.20.

THE BICYCLE DOG IN JUTLAND.

IN JUTLAND WITH A CYCLE

IN JUTLAND WITH A CYCLE

IN JUTLAND
WITH A CYCLE

BY

CHARLES EDWARDES

AUTHOR OF

'LETTERS FROM CRETE,' 'SARDINIA AND THE SARDES,'
'RIDES AND STUDIES IN THE CANARY ISLANDS,' ETC.

LONDON
CHAPMAN AND HALL, Ld.
1897

Richard Clay & Sons, Limited,
London & Bungay.

Dear "Sunbeam,"

As a novice in the art of understanding you, I played you a scurvy trick in thus taking you to a strange land; and further, as you are well aware, you were then hampered by the society of a pair of tyres little likely to bear with patience such trials as those I put upon you. But I have now become quite affectionately disposed towards you, since, in rougher lands than Denmark, you have unfolded to me, grown wiser, your many excellent qualities. In recognition whereof, I take leave to dedicate to your bright name this trivial record of our trivial journey together.

The Author.

CONTENTS

CHAPTER I

CHAPTER V

CHAPTER VI

CHAPTER VII

CHAPTER VIII

CHAPTER IX

CHAPTER X

CHAPTER XI

CHAPTER XII

CHAPTER XIII

CHAPTER XIV

CHAPTER XV

CHAPTER XVI

CHAPTER XVII

CHAPTER XVIII

CHAPTER XIX

IN JUTLAND WITH A CYCLE

CHAPTER I

Esbjerg — Fellow-travellers — A fellow-traveller — Rough quarters—A rough road—Dogs v. Cycle—Varde—Storks— A punctilious landlord.

I WAS last in Esbjerg in the great winter of 1892-3. Then its yellow sands were hid under the snow, and long icicles hung from its eaves. The ships in its roomy haven were stuck fast, and the hotels resounded with the grumbling voices of sea captains. It was only by herculean perseverance, and the good steel of the screw of the *Express,* that we had fought our way through the field of ice between Fanö and the mainland; not without exciting moments, mingled with cries from the engineer, and pardonable "language" from the captain. There were times in that struggle when we seemed doomed to be caught and gripped by the mighty floes crunching and groaning all about us. But in the end, after a ten hours' tussle to win through three miles of ice, we gained the battle, and steamed south with our bacon and butter.

It was so different now, in mid June. We glided smoothly over the blue water between the sand-heaps of north Fanö and the Skallingen headland, with the red roofs and yellow and white houses of Esbjerg plain before us. The North Sea had tossed us just a little in the night. The Danish young lady, travelling alone to her home in Zealand, had been ill, and I had not been very well. But there was scant excuse for our indisposition. So the flaxen-haired stewardess had told me as I lay in my berth reading *Trilby*, and breathing the sweet sea air of midsummer through my cabin window. Yet she failed to urge me out of my inertia. It were a shame to let the Danish young lady be solitary in her suffering.

There was an elderly Danish gentleman on board who had quite lately dined with the Lord Mayor of London. This fact came out casually while we were at luncheon. It has no value in itself, but it may lend a certain authority to his opinion about Esbjerg.

"It is a doll's town!" he said, with upheaved shoulders.

I remarked that it seemed to have grown considerably since the winter of 1892, and that its tricolor of red roofs and white bodies under so blue a sky was good to see.

"Yes," said he. "We sent you inhabitants once

upon a time; now we send you butter and pigs to keep your present inhabitants alive. Esbjerg lives on you. But it is a doll's town for all that—a ridiculous little place."

I was not so sure. Right opposite the harbour was a stately building with a dome. More south was another with a tower. These were Esbjerg's chief hotels. I remembered them both. In the former, three years ago, when it had no dome and much less body, I had spent an uneasy cold night under the short half of a feather-bed, and conceived a strong and doubtless unreasonable aversion for a fat little boy-man waiter, whose face always bore a mocking smile when I aired my Danish on him. They had both grown with the town itself. The population of the place had risen to ten thousand from about four thousand in 1890. Such progress would be creditable even in Matabeleland.

The Danish young lady and I went ashore together. We were both mere integers of humanity. It is nothing to the point that she was very pretty, with grey eyes, and the most charming English on her tongue. We had both suffered, and in the exchange of our experiences had become friendly. While I pushed my "Sunbeam" towards the Customs office, she walked by me and asked me which hotel I recommended. It was agreed that we would together see if the fat boy-man still condescended towards travellers at the domed building: she laughed as I limned him, and said she expected he was a Schleswiger. The Schleswigers do not, I imagine, excel in manners.

We were both soon free of the uniformed harpies. We left them prying industriously into the linen of a modest elderly English lady, who had crossed to Denmark under a botanical enthusiasm. They were vastly suspicious of the various tin cases that were to be filled with specimens.

My kindly companion would have intervened to explain things, and spare my countrywoman's blushes; but I stopped her. I urged that lessons are best learnt under the ferule of stern necessity. My countrywoman could not hope to collect floral specimens in Denmark without a tolerable knowledge of Danish. In the interests of her enthusiasm it were well, therefore, to leave her to grapple alone with this her first trial in the land. The Danish young lady's grey eyes did not seem quite to understand my argument; but she herself had heard of the New Woman, hated the species, and seemed willing to believe that a love of grasses was one of its many errors. We were both hard at work on Ibsen when we reached the domed hotel. Ibsen was one of my friend's fondest idols. And yet she loathed the New Woman!

This was a problem.

In the domed hotel they could not receive us, except at the dinner-table. We had delayed fatally in our walk over Esbjerg's yellow sands: our fellow-travellers were before us, and there were many to return by the steamer the next day. My friend insisted that they should find room for me; I learnt so much afterwards, and loved her for her unselfishness. But it was to no purpose.

Then came forth the florid, smiling landlord himself, and with him that little fat boy-man wretch (who knew me, though I was not now in furs, and had a cycle on my hands instead of a pair of skates), and they began a discussion. The upshot was, that the landlord led us to a mild, sequestered red house, with white curtains to the windows and a canary singing in the hall, and would have dumped us both on the people of the house with no regard for my dear friend's feelings. In the end she and I parted for the time. She was to sleep in the mild red house, and they were to fix up a casual bed for me in a concert room or something attached to the hotel. When she had had tea where she was, and I had dined at the hotel, we were to meet again for the long twilight of the June evening.

So it was. I sat next to a genial Copenhagen editor while I dined, and that fat boy-fool grinned at me over the dishes he brought. The editor was just at the end of a wild fit of locomotion. He had been to Rome, and Berlin, and London, and Edinburgh, and Heaven knows where else, and it had made him very happy. His English was just of a quality to incite me to sharpen my Danish on him; but alas! I resisted the opportunity. A better-natured man, I feel sure, there was not in all Denmark, but he brought confusion on my head by a vigorous inquiry if my wife was now quite recovered from the voyage, and by his subsequent loud merry laugh when he ascertained that the Danish young lady and I were not a newly-wedded couple on tour. And the way the boy-fool grinned into his hand, which had dirty nails!

However, another quarter of an hour and we were together again. Oh, these passing friendships! How lustily they grow in a minute or two, and then of a sudden the bladder is pricked as a "*Bon voyage*" or two are exchanged, the engine whistles, and with a handshake all is over.

Meanwhile we lived in the sunshine of the present. For two hours we strolled along the sands, with the North Sea rippling at the side, and the blue sky (which she thought so much bluer than England's) paling above us. At ten o'clock I saw her to her night's lodging. We were both to breakfast early, and be on the sands again the next day, there to stay until her accursed train started for the east.

From her I went into the Esbjerg theatre, which

adjoined the hotel, and saw some sickly grimacing. They had staged Ibsen. " Is not life sad ? " my friend had asked, when in our chatting I had protested against the dolor of the Scandinavian sage's conclusions, and I had made her smile as I told her that it all depended upon the eyes through which you looked at it.

I expected fleas that night, and felt them. The room was of that gigantic size you sometimes discover in a small country, with dusty curtains fifty or a hundred feet high to the row of windows, through which I could not keep the daylight, which at this time of the year in Denmark glimmers even in the witching hours. About eight vast doors let upon my chamber. They all opened either when I was in bed or dressing the next morning. One moment a shock-headed seafaring man, the next a smart *handelsmand*, then a maidservant, and, of course, the boy-fool—each in turn passed through me to somewhere else. The night was warm notwithstanding, and so was the blue feather-bed I lay three parts under.

The morning, however, atoned for all. When I turned out, the sky was blithely blue and white, and the sands were like spilt gold dust. The North Sea was curling tiny waves upon the sand, and two terrible women were bathing in them, naked from the waist upwards. Towards the north-west, I saw

the first of those quaint landscape cheats with which
I was to become familiar in Jutland. In the clear
air, far away, white shapes and black shapes stood
up on the horizon line like ships. The shrewdest
eye could detect no connecting base of land for
them, yet they were houses and churches, set about
one foot only above the level of the sea.

The Danish young lady said she had slept well.
Her pretty face testified to her words. From nine
o'clock until twelve we idled on the sands together.
In that time I believe I obtained as true an idea of
her sweet soul as any one, save herself, might obtain,
not excepting her father. Some of our words are
not to be echoed. From rather profound sentiment we shot up of a sudden to the trivial surfaces
of life. In one of these petty moments, she wrote in
my pocket-book the Danish for "woollen quilts,"
having pitied me for my feather-bed woe of the past
night. We had brief bouts of exercise in pronun-
ciation, and charming little wrinkles arose on her
forehead when I proved a fool of a pupil. Then off
she would go into the depths of gravity, as thus:
"When I was at Eton the other day, with my
brother, I was wondering about all those little boys.
Is it not enough to make thought? They will be
great men of State, or soldiers like my father, or
what besides. But now they are only little boys
with very polite manners, at least to me." Nothing

much in this, you will say. Ah, but her voice, pretty face, and reflective grey eyes sublimed everything. We parted when the train left for Copenhagen, and I cast my hopes of eventual reunion upon the future.

Now that I was alone, I turned my thoughts towards my "Sunbeam," which had meanwhile leaned lazily against the colour-washed wall of Mr. Spangsberg's hotel. Esbjerg was insufferable without my friend. It is but a poor little new place at the best, though with shops above the common for Denmark. Its streets were deep rutted; half-developed houses abounded; I heard the yells of suspicious swine in the pig-slaughtery; and there was now no one to come between me and my landlord's discomforting head waiter. I had talked English hitherto, but now I was veritably a stranger in a strange land, and the realization irked me.

Whoever looked on my cycle admired it. In the hotel hall it had its bell rung many times by sympathetic Danes, old and young. I had heard the music while I dressed in my big room and while I breakfasted. One youth waylaid me to inquire about its value, and went off with a long face when I told him the truth. Another wished badly that I should try its speed against his machine; but I had no heart for such ostentatious achievements. I wished to be free of Esbjerg, and free to move as I pleased. And so I paid my bill, saw my portmanteau labelled "Skagen," and mounted. My landlord and two or three others wished me well, having warned me of the quality of the western roads, and I shot away from them. Varde was my destination; the distance some eleven and a half miles, the direction due north, the wind westerly.

I was soon in the wilds. Having passed the last suburban house of Esbjerg, I had brown moor on both sides of me, broken here and there by farmsteads, with small green patches close around them. The wind sang cheerily over this healthy treeless stretch, and larks sang with the wind. Off and on from the different low-browed farmhouses dogs of no exalted strain, but of great size, dashed barking towards me, taking the moorland mounds with most offensive leaps. Once I had four of them about my wheels and legs, snapping and egging each other on in their diverting enterprise. A countryman, with a rake in one hand and his pipe-bowl in the other, stood on a ridge and watched for the consequences. Only when I had measured my length, and spilled my "Sunbeam" on his mongrel, did he seem satisfied. By then, however, I had taken my defence upon myself, and routed the dogs with some of the large pebbles which lay ready to hand on the chopped-up road.

These experiences recurred. Furthermore, the

road deteriorated. It narrowed so that it was little better than two ruts with a pebbly ridge between. A degraded footway ran alongside, some twelve inches wide, and cleft every twenty yards or so by a drainage cutting. A ditch with nice black ooze in it (and lilies on the ooze where it broadened) lay beneath the footway, to inspire confidence. Such was the thoroughfare between Esbjerg and Varde. When I crossed the railway I was nearly resolved to wait for a train, and signal to it to stop and pick me up. But I did no such thing, and in about two hours, after a deal of trundling, I came to the high-road between Varde and Ribe, with Varde's spire in a hollow beyond, and a surprising little wood. The remaining two miles were faultless, and brought me to the Varde river, which I could see zigzagging east and west through meadows as green and lush as ever delighted a cow.

Varde's main street climbed from the bridge, and, like the streets of all Danish towns, was stoutly paved. I was thankful the hotel Dania was near at hand, though it was yet far enough up to make me an object of interest in the town. The Danes love to enliven their placid existence with small cross mirrors fastened outside their windows. Thus aged and decrepit dames, far set in their chambers, can without effort see all who go and come in the streets. One or two of these ancients were not content thus to view my "Sunbeam" at a distance. They shuffled to their windows, and showed their white-capped heads to the world.

Having stabled my steed and fixed the supper hour, I went forth into Varde's pleasant meadows by the river-side. There was nothing better to do; certainly nothing more exciting, unless I went to the pig-slaughtery. But I was perfectly content thus to saunter and smoke among forget-me-nots, butter-cups, and ragged robin, with the brown stream slouching steadily to the sea by my side. There were cuckoos in the trees, and the larks kept up their chant. Here, too, I saw my first stork, a gaunt, red-beaked object, with hanging red legs. It dropped in a coal-yard over against the railway station. East of the bridge some young storks were paddling in the shallows, not at all disturbed by the two or three Varde children who paddled near them. The gaunt object seemed to be engaged in stuffing the youngsters with bits of coal, or else I grievously misunderstood her various voyages.

Close by the bridge was something quite as sug-gestive as the storks—a rounded low grassy hill, to wit. There was no doubting its purpose. An early Jute of distinction had here been buried; perhaps the first lord of Varde, which, unlike Esbjerg, can boast of centuries of recorded history. I looked with interest at the mound, little knowing how I was to be surfeited with others like it, and I wondered if the dead gentleman had in his day sailed down the river to the fiord of Hjerting, and thence made the trip to Kent. Like enough he did so, and has relations now living in Deal or Dover.

Under the warm June sun, and facing the west wind, these Varde river-side meadows were good to plod in. I left them for my hotel with regret. Here I found my landlord awaiting me with some formality. The table was spread, and he was clad most genteelly. He drank my health in schnapps as a prelude, and then, with his own hands, helped me to the smoked salmon, dried herring, ham, tongue, eels, mutton and beef, which confused me with their various charms. He would not eat with me, being satisfied to entertain me with his conversation, evidently glad of a guest, and perhaps particularly pleased to house an Englishman. My countryfolk are not much seen in Varde, but Varde, like all Denmark, respects us as consumers of its produce. That, I judge, was why, afterwards, the dear man introduced me to every one as "the Englishman!" when, at his earnest invitation, I consented to be led about to view the glories of Varde. He even took me into a small tobacconist's shop on no other pretext, so that I was fain to relieve the social tension by purchasing a dozen cigars.

Ere this we had spent a discreet half-hour over

coffee in a tiny arbour in the garden, with a stork's nest on a chimney-pot hard by. I would willingly have stayed with the stork, but for the gold-headed cane my landlord had brought forth, and his repeated hints that Varde expected to be visited. And so we stumbled up and down the cobbled streets, and the honest man unbonneted to every mother's son we clashed with, and gave them greeting. He irritated me in other ways. When I thrust both my hands into my breeches pockets he did likewise, carrying his cane under his arm. When, for a change, I put my right hand in the small of the back, his broad back also required support. He walked precisely as I walked, now with short steps, and now striding. And so on. It was laughable enough, however, and of course but another kindly tribute to his guest's excellence.

We walked out to the Varde *skov*, or wood, and through the Varde cemetery, with its pathetic little marble doves on marble slabs, and brief mortuary inscriptions of farewell. The red western sky made the wood more romantic than it is; and so did the betrothed couples who moved with quiet footfalls up and down its slim alleys. My landlord was heartless enough to intrude upon the privacy of one of these couples, just to make me known to the gentleman. The young lady, meanwhile, turned her face to the west, which outdid her cheeks in colour. I earned her gratitude, I do hope, by the abruptness with which I cut short this uncalled-for interview.

The "sick-house," the schools, the burgermaster's abode, and the church were all shown to me, and Frederic the Seventh's martial statue in the broad cobbled square, with some lively boys and girls playing at touch round about it. My companion deftly caught one of these maidens by her flaxen pigtail, and for a moment I feared yet another formal introduction was to come. But he meant only to show me her face, which he reckoned, he said, as pretty as any in Varde. The maiden, however, did not appreciate the compliment. She put forth her tongue at him most valorously, and the boys hooted, so that my landlord felt forced to let her slip. I gave that damsel a twenty-öre piece, by no means because of her beauty, and then proclaimed my drowsiness with all the speech I could muster.

In some countries they will not understand that a man goes to an inn quite as much to be left to himself, as because he needs a bed and a supper. But they are a primitive people in Jutland, with obsolete ideas of hospitality.

CHAPTER II

Sunday on the road—A desolate district—Lyne—Tarm—
Skjern and its revivalists—Bad going—Ringkjöbing and
the fiord— Storks at home—Sunday night in the provinces
—Young bloods of Ringkjöbing.

My Varde bed was irreproachable, and so was the
coffee which my landlord himself brought me just
before seven o'clock the next morning. There had
been rain in the night—the glisten of it was bright
on the roofs opposite.

"You shall have showers," said my host, who, on
little or no invitation, stayed while I made my toilet,
and dodged the eyes of an inquisitive dame at a
window level with mine across the narrow street.
"But," he hastened to add, "it will not be much
rain, and the wind is good."

At half-past seven I was ready to be off. The
rolling of wheels in the rough street long ago had
told me I was none too early for my reputation's
sake. It was Sunday, and the stout wains that came
into Varde were packed with sturdy Jutlanders,
men and women, wearing church-going countenances.

16

The ladies held their psalm books under their shawls out of the rain, while their stolid husbands, brothers, and cousins smoked their festival pipes, long things with bowls the size of a decent fist, and painted with garish landscapes or uncouth human countenances.

Every Danish village of consequence has its cycle smith, and every town its half-dozen of them. Before starting up the street, we visited the Varde smith to get his health certificate. It was obvious, Sabbath or not, that he would be tempted by such weakness, and he required a quarter of an hour to rectify a stiffness of the pedals. Then I turned my back on the hotel Dania, and, escorted by my landlord, made for the suburbs. The paved road in the town's precincts was not fit to ride on. Moreover, it was at a fairish gradient, and made me the less disposed to become a spectacle for the haberdashers, the bakers, the wood-turners, and tub-makers who stood at their doors with sleek honest faces, and, for all their gentle courtesies, would have called lustily to their wives and children to share the fun, had I spilt myself on the Varde stones before their eyes.

"Farewell, Herr Englishman, and a fortunate journey!" said my landlord, when an endless stretch of high-road appeared before me.

I mounted and rode forth from the town, its red roofs, its pale yellow and white houses, and its

c

massive church with the tall spire. The air was fresh, and though the sky was thickly bespread with puffed cloud-shapes, there was sunlight enough to give me hope. Ringkjöbing was my goal; the distance thirty-seven miles. I had all the day at my disposal, so that West Jutland would have plenty of time to make its native mark on my mind.

Here again I was no sooner out of the town than I was in the moorlands. The telegraph wire, which was to move with me until the evening, ran from post to post set among the heather and bluebells. West I could see nothing but this russet moor, with low farmsteads dotted about; east the same, though the sky-line here was black with rain; and north was the moor again to the farthest undulation. My road was about as straight as a ruler, though not at all level.

For the first hour I enjoyed a succession of brief adventures in the passage of the various wagons taking the rustics into Varde. The carts were drawn by handsome huge horses, decked with bells and rather gay harness gear. These looked as little likely as the Sphinx to be troubled by nerves. Yet no sooner did I glide quietly towards them— well to the right, which is Denmark's rule of the road—than they acted as if possessed. If the wagon had two horses, as most of them had, up rose the two pairs of forelegs high into the air. The women screamed, as women will even now-a-days in the country, and embraced each other and those next them. But the Jutland men bore the trial with admirable phlegm: they did not so much as take their hands from their pipe bowls. Like as not, the driver saluted me with one hand while he held his reins with the other. The struggle was brief, and ere I could look round all was composed. They do not see many cycles in West Jutland; hence all this fuss.

As for the rosy-cheeked boys and girls wending their way to Sunday school (or I hope so), they showed reverence towards me and my "Sunbeam." While yet I was afar off they drew up in line by the roadside; then the little maids dropped pretty curtseys, and their brothers uncovered their heads— all in dead silence.

But I soon came to an end of such road mates, and there were miles when I had nothing in sight but the humpy moor, the clouds, and the telegraph wires. As I expected, the road grew rapidly worse the farther I left Varde behind; and so did the weather. I had to fight fitful gusts which wailed in front from the north instead of steadily on the quarter. And betimes the clouds joined issue right overhead, and damped me with very earnest showers. But they were nothing worse than showers, which

soon dried up, and brought out the perfume
of the bog-myrtle about the wet hollows, where
silvery little pools reflected the ardent clouds, and
told no tales about the coal-black peaty mud their
waters covered. And rain, wind, or sunshine, the
larks carolled amazingly over the barren land, and
were as lusty a tonic for the mind as was the
bustling west wind for the lungs.

I passed divers tombs of the vikings this morning, symmetrical mounds set in the loneliness by
twos and threes, and saw many others in the distance, but chiefly in the east, where the outlook was
downright desolation in its black treelessness. By
one of them, when I had gone for an hour, I lay
down on the heather and smoked a pleasant pipe,
while the heat vapour rose all round me, and ran
before the wind. And here I lay day-dreaming for
nearly another hour, while a light shower or two fell
on my radiant "Sunbeam" (lolling against a telegraph post), and beaded it with diamantine rain-
drops. And no one passed all that time.

It was nearly ten miles before I came to a village.
This was Lyne. It consisted of two or three roomy
farmsteads, a school-house, and a granite church with
a saddle tower, mercilessly whitewashed. I hit the
place towards church time. Two elderly dames in
black, with black kerchiefs over their heads, had
just entered the churchyard, and a girl with mouse-

coloured stockings to her long legs stood by the wall, holding her prayer-book while she watched me. This poor child seemed more than alarmed when I ran my cycle up to her to rest it where she stood, and her mouse-coloured legs hurried to the church door at a trot. I heard a somnolent chant from inside, which told of service begun. For this reason I did not join the congregation, though I tarried fully a minute in the white porch with an old woman whom I had seen carry a small nosegay of flowers in a paper bag to a little grave hard by, having previously tossed away, with considerable petulance, the withered flowers it was to supersede. The dame sniffed loudly while we kept company, and tweaked her nose at the extremity with forefinger and thumb in the oddest manner (as if to silence it); but as I had nothing to say to her she went in at length, giving me a brief glimpse of a number of parted mouths and wandering eyes. The church was as white within as without.

There was nothing to delay for in Lyne, and so I rode on. In the courtyard of one of the farms three heavy young men were playing croquet, each with a cumbrous pipe in his mouth. All the church-goers had seen them at their pastime, and the pastor to boot. But the Lutheran system is very tolerant of such human frailties, and there was doubtless no scandal about the proceeding.

Between Lyne and Tarm (some seven miles farther) the road became abominable—a fell mixture of pebbles, ruts, and sand. Uphill or downhill, the experience was galling. I trundled for about an hour, rocketing over the big pebbles between-whiles, and thereby qualifying for eternal immunity from liver disease. But at Tarm, which won esteem by a very large mill close to the road, there was a sudden change for the better. Two miles to the north is the station village of Skjern, with a church and two or three thousand souls; and these two miles of road, across a delta of the much-muddled river Skjern, were as good as any that ever consoled a weary cyclist for past trials.

Though but a tiny place, Tarm appeared, from its name-boards, to have representatives of all the usual trades and petty industries. But it has no inn and no church. I met its inhabitants returning from worship in Skjern, and I must say they stared a great deal. They looked quite uninteresting in their Sabbath black, and the men moved with that curious curving swing forward of the leg so noticeable in some of our own rheumaticky rustics.

The river Skjern is a sprawling important drain for the marshes to the east. I crossed four of its arms in deep muddy beds, with broad lily leaves on the sluggish thick water; and then, with the white saddle of Skjern's church close at hand, and the railway line alongside, rode into the village, which seemed remarkably populous, and alighted at the larger of its two guest-houses. Almost simultaneously a drum was banged, and I understood what the crowd meant by the railway station opposite the inn. The Salvation Army was trying its hand on Skjern, and the Skjern villagers, with pipes in their mouths, were listening with impartial demeanour to a hymn just started by two intelligent-looking girls in the familiar poke-bonnet. The road here was very wide, and hundreds of other Jutlanders, of all ages and both sexes, were patrolling up and down. It was Skjern's Church Parade.

I have little idea of the current worth in Denmark of meat and drink, but I should like to bear testimony to the cheapness of the Skjern inn, according to British standards. My bill was two crowns, which is two shillings and threepence. For this they fed me on beef and potatoes, with meal jelly, sugar and cream, Gruyère cheese, butter, bread, and two bottles of Carlsberg beer. Coffee and schnapps may be added, and also about half-a-pint more schnapps for my flask. The meal was homely but contenting; and so was my treatment in the place, when once I had made my wants known to the spectacled old lady who seemed to own the inn. The sympathetic soul offered me her drawing-room to smoke in after dinner, with Leipzig prints on the walls. She had previously made arrangements of a more surprising kind. I had babbled somewhat of fatigue, due to the roads, whereupon she had sped her maid with the warming-pan to one of the beds. And no sooner was dinner over than she led me by the arm (holding her Bible in the other hand) to the bed-chamber, and turned down its sheets. But I was not all that weary. Her bare sofa contented me, and the photographs on the table of herself, as a little unspectacled maid, and a number of stiff-bearded and aggressive young men in pea-jackets, whom I take to have been the lovers that years ago fought for her favour. But those stalwart days were long past, and now, on Sunday afternoons, she reads her Bible when she is not serving customers at the bar, and remembers only vaguely the joys of Church Parade and her bodyguard of suitors.

From Skjern the road continued towards Ringkjöbing with extreme straightness. It was sufficiently good for a mile or two, and then its old roughness reappeared. Hereabouts I was confronted by a really pretentious hill, for West Jutland. The whitish seam climbed to the dun-coloured ridge at a very respectable angle, and a conspicuous funereal pimple kept guard on the west side of the summit. On this eminence I hoped for a wide and lively view; but instead of that I saw only the endless moor with its

many farmsteads, and some three or four white
churches. I was level with the spacious Ringkjöbing
Fiord, and barely five miles from it, but could make
out nothing of it.

The rain swooped down while I halted thus
by the eleventh Danish milestone from Ribe. I
had to seek shelter among the scrub and juniper
on the viking's tomb. Its crest was sunken, so
that it resembled a baby volcano; and there were
scars on its side, which hinted at the prowls of
antiquaries.

Hence, until I joined the great main east road
between Ringkjöbing and Herning, I enjoyed much
diversity of level, so that Jutland rose in my esteem.
Some of the ancient farmhouses were almost stately,
and their appointments always impressed by their
trimness. A manor or two also reminded me, that
though Jutland is now a country given up to the
tenant-farmer, class distinctions are not dead here.
Holmgaard was the most noticeable of these
dwellings, with a fine outlook towards the fiord,
and on the other side of the road the towerless
granite church of St. Lem, more like a dignified barn
than a church. The country was still devoid of
trees—an unresisting prey to the wild west winds.
But there were plenty of meadow patches, with kine
tethered among the clover, and unambitious men
and women sitting near, counting the mouthfuls

eaten by the cattle; and a fair number of dogs, who showed keen interest in my "Sunbeam."

So to the junction, where it behoved me to face the breeze and a road quite consecrated to ruts. Cycling was here well-nigh impossible. In fact, for the last four miles into Ringkjöbing I was mainly a pedestrian, and an uncomfortable one too. The white tower of Rindum church, near my haven, and the spire of the church of Ringkjöbing, were a terrible time in becoming adequately near. But I reached the pleasant suburbs at length, crossed the railway, and ran into the heart of the town's paved ways. Sabbath silence brooded over the place, and some of the perfumes from its own gutters and the fiord shores were both powerful and pungent.

Ringkjöbing as I saw it soothed the soul much like Varde's flowery meadows. I left my cycle at the hotel, with the thick little trees shadowing its long line of windows, and made for the town's enclosed area of salt water. My nose led me thither unerringly. What tide there may be here was at its lowest, and I had to step across Ringkjöbing's bare-faced sewers one by one, while I skirted the water to the south. The sky was angry—black and gold where the sun was, and over the all but invisible sand bay of land, six or seven miles across the fiord (its western boundary), unadulterated stormy black. In all, the fiord may be sixteen or seventeen miles

long by an average of six miles wide—a tolerably
pretentious though shallow inland lake. In time it
will presumably be drained, and its narrow sinuous
outlet to the south be dammed. But the artist will
hardly forgive the capitalists who thus rob Ringkjöbing of its picturesqueness.

The little red-roofed town stands some eight or
nine feet above the fiord, with sand and reeds for a
shore. Outside the town precincts the land forms
pretty infantine cliffs of red earth and sand. A
bold boy would jump from the top of the loftiest
of them. Still, they are not to be despised, and
in their hollows is good herbage, with sheep
and lambs tied, so that they must eat every
edible blade of grass within a radius of about nine
feet.

The fiord underwent many moods during the hour
or two I gave to it. Now it was a placid pool of
silver, and the sail of the small boat that was crossing
it to the Holmsland Cape lay flat against the mast.
Then the ripple would rise far to the west, the boys in
the boat bestirred themselves, and they tacked fast to
the north-west; while, a little later, I was almost
blown into the poppied cornfield that ran from the
cliff tops east. The white saddle tower of the church
of Gammel Sogns close on the north shore of the fiord
looked well in the picture, with the wild crimson and
black of the clouds behind it. Swallows swished

about the fiord sands, and the larks were as energetic as ever above the cornfields.

I was told that Ringkjöbing is the home of dozens of retired sea-captains. A knot of bronzed men with a telescope were gathered on the tiny pier, where the smells were most fervent, and I dare say these were some of them. They might end their days in a worse place, though they must surely often wish that mile-broad strip of land in the distance was not between them and the North Sea with its ships. But when the drainers come here, as they have already reached the Stadil Fiord just to the north, and connected with Ringkjöbing Fiord, the sea-captains will assuredly up anchor and be off. An island like Fanö will be more to their taste, and they will there find plenty of their brethren, with green parrots pendant in the parlours, and corals and shells galore on the tables and mantels, and yarns true or less true of adventurous voyages far north and south in little ships of the old style.

Ringkjöbing's hotel feasted me on the customary assortment of cold slices, with hot stewed eels as the dish of the day. There is something fiendishly embarrassing about the Danish *koldt bord*, as this service of cold slices is called. Among so many excellent attractions one knows not how to choose, nor exactly when to stop. But I suppose habit is the great instructor here as elsewhere.

I found a most delightful housetop in view from the hotel coffee-room—a roof with two chimneys to it and a stork's nest. In the nest was a family of young storks, and a devoted mother stork was perched on the edge of the rough mass of sticks in the hollow of which her children lay—restlessly enough, if I might judge by the frequent extrusion of their red noses. The gentleman stork for long stood listless on the adjacent chimney-pot. He was evidently not wanted at home, nor did he seem particularly anxious to get nearer his family. Once when I thought him fast asleep he scratched his beak meditatively with his red leg. A little later he turned round and viewed his wife and children, and then took to flight. Madame stork didn't seem to mind ; she stayed where she was, and only occasionally thrust her beak into the nest, as if she were gently settling Master Tom or Miss Jane for the night's repose. Suddenly back came the gentleman stork, with what looked like a fish. Now, methought, for a touching illustration of unselfishness, a lesson from a creature low in the scale of development to one vastly well up in the scale. But, bless your soul, it was nothing of the kind. The old glutton swallowed the fish very methodically, without giving his wife so much as a glance at it. Then, when he had gulped two or three times, as if to dispose of a prickly fin or a bone, he hopped sharply to the nest, made a distinct fuss,

clawed the sticks this way and that, ordered his wife
to lie down, and finally settled on the top of her. It
was slightly dusk by this time, so I may have
misinterpreted certain of his actions; but the main
incidents are as I describe them. His red nose ran
out over the sticks at the side like a cannon on a
fort, and nothing much else of the whole family was
to be seen.

While this comedy was being enacted, the gay
male gentlefolk of Ringkjöbing stole into the coffee-
room one by one and began to toss dice. They did
it rather diffidently, it seemed to me, as if they
thought it a breach of good manners not to invite me
into their game. But they were not at all diffident
in their treatment of the waiter—a humble and very
intelligent young man, who understood every word of
my Danish. Him they clamoured at, first for one
thing and then for another, and they bullied him
right well, so that he looked quite tearful. And
afterwards again they glanced at me, and it was as
plain as the spoon in my coffee cup that they wished
me to perceive what a fine appreciation they had of
the requirements as well as the manners of metropolitan existence. Their faces spoke for them. "See
what first-rate men of the world we are, though we
do live just at present in such a hole-and-corner
place as this!"

Outside, even up to half-past ten, the square between the portly church tower base and the hotel was populous with young men and young women, talking and laughing in the twilight. There was much lifting of hats, and there were alluring pigtails of many hues. In towns like Copenhagen, Denmark has theatres for its people on Sunday evenings; but in Denmark's provinces the inhabitants must be content with what Sabbath sport their somewhat inactive minds can evoke from their barren circumstances. I asked the humble waiter if there was dancing that evening.

"No, sir," he answered promptly; "we are always very quiet in Ringkjöbing."

Whereupon the braggart dice-players, who had listened with all their ears to my inquiry and its reply, cast glowering looks at the waiter. "To give us away like that!" they said with their eyes; "it's perfectly shameful!" One of them ordered some cognac, and, having pushed a halfpenny extra towards the poor young man, changed his mind and reclaimed the coin. I would have wagered more than the halfpenny that this was his way of punishing the waiter for the indiscretion of his tongue.

CHAPTER III

THE country north-east of Ringkjöbing is almost as
dreary as any in Jutland; nor is its tameness relieved
by undulations, rivers, or a suggestive number of
vikings' tombs. Our ancient heroes had a fine
knack of choosing their sepulchres, or having them
chosen, in spots of quite repulsive ugliness; but they
seem to have found this part of the Ringkjöbing
Amt too unattractive even to be burnt on after
death.

This, my third day in Jutland, was doomed to be
calamitous and humiliating to my "Sunbeam."

We started fair, in sunshine, though with a thick
pack of clouds scudding over the town from the
North Sea. My friends the storks made an ominous
cluttering quite early; and while I dressed, within
half a stone's throw of their mansion, I beheld something like a scene of domestic strife in the nest. It

32

ended in the male stork majestically lifting his legs in the air and making for the shore of the fiord. He must have been a sad wretch of a husband and father, for no sooner was he gone (to stuff his own grey stomach) than peace reigned, and the good housewife arranged her plumage at her ease, as often as not balanced to a marvel on but one of her red legs. Periodically, however, she examined the sky. She seemed to have her doubts about the day.

And she was right. I left the Ringkjöbing hotel at half-past eight, after a short survey of the church, which is a whitewashed brick monster, qualified to congeal a man's religion in his soul. My cycle gave me no anxiety at the start. True, the tyres had been somewhat tried in those rampaging runs over great pebbles between Esbjerg and Skjern, and they needed air with some frequency; but I had no idea their constitution had become seriously affected.

Yet when I was clear of the town's clean pavements, and was moving excellently on a comfortable incline towards the distant church of Hee, I felt something happen. The jolts continued. Then I stopped, and found the hind tyre flat and empty. A man with two very tame cows encouraged me while I pumped. But the pumping was vain; and so, with moderate haste, I proceeded to push back into the town, nearly a mile and a half distant. Here, after brief coquetting with the cycle smith,

the tyre consented to take breath, and away we sped
again, I by this time a little anxious, for the clouds
certainly meant business, and I was on a road with a
great dearth of inns or places of shelter. If I could
get to the church of Hee before the first shower,
that, methought, would do.

But again, when I had gone about two miles, the
tyre flattened itself out, and impatience seized me.
Down came the rain also. I invaded a farmyard,
and in an odorous cowshed my "Sunbeam" and I
waited, listening to the flogging of the rain on the
roof till we had exhausted the dregs of our patience.
Afterwards, to the astonishment of the cattle, who
had joined us in the shed, we went out in the rain,
and I had the wet and melancholy task of trundling
yet again back to Ringkjöbing. The day looked of
settled badness. It were foolish to ride in such
weather. To the station therefore we hied, and,
very damp and wounded, we took tickets for Skive,
some forty-eight miles north-east. To occupy the
interval on our hands, we did as other waiting
countryfolk did, and ordered coffee and gin at the
humble refreshment bar. The luxury cost three-
halfpence, and was not so much amiss as it sounds.

In Denmark, whatever other faults they possess,
they never risk your neck on the railway. The
trains are uniformly slow except near to Copenhagen.
They are very slow in Jutland. There is, too, such

an elaborate official mechanism for the safeguard of
passengers. Thus, before a train is allowed to start,
electric bells tinkle one after the other, telling of the
clearness of the line up to a certain station. This
sort of thing continues for the thorough warning of
passengers. It is "one, two, three," and only then
"away." Finally, the station-master, a magnificent
personage, with a chest, and one hand thrust im-
posingly into his double-breasted coat of crimson
and gold, with the other hand strikes the clapper
of a common bell. This is the departure signal.
Having given it, the gentleman retires indoors
with the air of a general who has achieved a
victory. The station-master is by far the handsomest
object at a Danish station for those who are interested
in manly swagger; but I fancy the alert young
ladies who do the secretarial work in his offices, and
glance up with dainty wrinkles of anxiety on their
foreheads as each train rumbles in, are the real
machinery of the place. Their lord and master rings
the bell, and stands now and then with his chin in
his hand contemplating the prettiest of his slaves
while she writes. I have seldom seen the gentleman
strain himself worse than that. He will, however,
if you accost him, talk with you most affably; and,
though I laugh at him, as a whole I like him. He
and his colleagues are most soldierly in appearance.
They are often, indeed, transformed warriors; the

Danish railways being State property, the State rewards her veterans with these agreeable little sinecures.

It rained with fury all the way to Skive. The journey lasted exactly four hours, which is a mile in five minutes, including the pauses at Holstebro and Struer, both lengthy.

I saw the church of Hee from the train, and wished I could prudently have alighted to examine it. Its short tower and high roof, with the gabled windows to its apse, differed much from the conventional parish church of Jutland. But, of course, its granite was whitewashed. This monstrous habit may perhaps be explained by the old necessity for landmarks in this desolate region. There is no missing the snow-white little buildings which dot the bleak ridges and the boggy plains; whereas the normal grey or pale red of the granite commonly used would often blend imperceptibly with the mists and clouds begotten by the North Sea, and volleyed over the land. But now that the old conditions of life have departed in Jutland, and there are roads of a sort everywhere, not to mention railways, the good pastors may be respectfully urged to join issue and combat the great god whitewash, whose sway in their parishes is fully as pagan as anything their worthy ancestors bowed the knee to a thousand years or so ago.

There was a decent man in the train, who, having experimented on me with a Danish newspaper, and subsequently cross-examined me, to learn if my perusal of it was all a sham, of a sudden spoke English as good as my own. He had in his day been to Hull and Grimsby. His trade was fat beasts. A blunt-spoken honest fellow with a red beard, and in his pocket a French novel. This last he laid on the seat, for no reason in particular except that I might see it. He had also a memorandum book, in which he made calculations with one eye shut. The other eye he used quite as much for me as for his figures. It drew my attention to the manor-house of Nörre Vosborg, among trees close to the line, one of the handsomest in the province. But the blur of rain spoiled all; even made the brown moor, with its interspaces of swamp and patches of black, chopped peat land, more dismal than it would else have been.

Holstebro and Struer were nothing to me but two agitated crowds of men with pipes, and caps rammed on their heads so as to set their largish ears sticking out laterally. This must be the accepted local way of wearing the cap. Without prejudice it cannot be recommended, though it may have acoustic advantages about which I am ignorant.

It had turned cold in all this rain. There was no enduring an open window, and my companions smoked that strong rough tobacco which alone suits their long-stemmed, great-bowled pipes.

At Struer we were on the shore almost at the extreme southern point of that spacious waterway which divides Jutland from east to west, and makes an island of the Hjörring Amt, the Skaw being its extreme north point. This most intricate of fiords or inland seas ought to be picturesque. But the absence of mountains or even hills of any magnitude handicaps it. The islands that lie about it are, again, far more piquant on the map than in fact. Many of them are only a foot or two above the water at high tide, and half their area is then expunged. This inland sea is called the Lim Fiord in the north, where it resembles a ship canal. But its southern reaches are known as *bredningen*, or broads. I must confess that I was disappointed with it, though I ought not to have expected great things from so flat a country as Jutland.

Between Struer and Skive the train skirted the Venö Bay of this enclosed sea. A murky haze was over it, and did not dignify it. Then we struck across the base of the peninsula which separates the Venö Bay from the Skive Fiord—a hilly district for Jutland. But though hilly, there was precious little beauty in its scenes. Even the extensive Flynder Lake, by which we run for about four miles, looked what it was and nothing more, namely, a big pool of rain-water between long ridges of treeless moor, the ridges mournfully uniform, and, at the most, a hundred and fifty feet above the water. In the wet hollows of these Jutland highlands were a myriad of little stacks of coal-black peat; and at the railway stations hereabouts peats by the hundred thousand were stored, or in cars ready to be transported to the towns. That country is in a bad way which has to live, so to speak, on its own skin.

I was glad to alight at the Skive station.

Here was something much better. We were at the tip of a fiord; there was also a river of size, which ran darkly into the fiord, having drained the dismal Alhede district to the south, and also being connected with the Flynder Lake. The town is on a hill to one side of the fiord, and, under the flash of sunlight that now obligingly followed the rain, looked both sparkling and clean. Factories near the station betokened it a place of industry, and the blacksmiths by the road into it were merrily clinking at their irons.

It was quite a steep climb for my disabled "Sunbeam," which I had declined to entrust to the porter of the Gluds Hotel. But I might have spared the poor thing the ascent, for the smith who was to mend it lived in the lowlands. Meanwhile, they received me at the hotel in fluent English, with sympathetic condolences about the weather and prompt mention of dinner. I had long overpassed the conventional dinner hour (one or thereabouts), thanks to my snail of a train; but I was not to suffer for a State failing. Landlord, head-waiter, and the cook himself all came to discuss the matter. It was as if I were the leading butter merchant in the world, instead of a wet vagabond of a cyclist. But, as will have been surmised, in Denmark they respect the man on a machine much more than the average Briton may be said to respect him. The ostlers at the hotels stable his steed with a certain reverence, and the railway porters handle it admiringly, with the utmost regard for its parts.

The fried sole they served me in one corner of the large dining-room here was soon despatched, and I went out to view Skive and its neighbourhood. Inclination drew me towards the fiord, but my legs selected the wrong way, and it was only after a long round that I struck a road leading through a gay little *skov* towards the water. This *skov* altogether beat Varde's for its foliage and grassy dells with seats in them, and its band-stand and wet tables for tea-drinking and "bocks" on gala occasions. There were rose-bushes all in flower in it and a fountain or two. Quite a pretty little town wood indeed, and warranted to attune the hearts of young men and maids for amorous whispers and junketings.

I wonder who started this rage for woods in Denmark. Was it some portly burgermaster with a houseful of daughters, whose ordinary faces were not marketable under the common conditions of social intercourse? Whether this was their origin, or whether (as is more likely) the passion has come down from the time of Odin, the vogue is a very pleasing one. The chroniclers tell us how, in the famous grove by Old Upsala, dead men might have been seen hanging from the trees in honour of the three divinities who consecrated the place. The modern Scandinavians devote their groves to worthier rites and sacrifices.

Having passed through the wood, I skirted a small wild hanging forest, with yellow iris by fifties in the watery ditch at its base, and so came to Skive's port and pier. A Copenhagen steamboat was taking cargo for departure on the morrow, and a knowing mariner in a blue jersey, and with a spirituous nose, was inviting three or four timid adventurers to smell the fish he was unpacking from a box.

One of those comical old ladies in black caps and with disgracefully short frocks, for which Jutland seems remarkable, came out at me from a small house with green shutters by the pier head, and asked if I wanted a bath. The idea was not unwelcome, yet, after meditation, I declined the enterprise. But when I was on the pier I understood.

A modest arrangement of boards was here run out into the quiet, all-but-stagnant waters of the fiord, and the word "Baths" was on it. Some shrill sounds and splashings were audible from the ladies' side of the erection. In truth, though, the air was altogether too cool thus to plunge unprepared into such water, which had a scum on it that I hope was not due wholly to the bathers.

The fiord stretched to the north in a widening arm, with faint grey land in the distance. It was so still that it made me yawn to look at it. A mile across it from the pier were unassuming treeless green and brown hills, with the inevitable white church on the ridge summit. A few gulls and very many excited daddy-long-legs were the other main ingredients of a picture that was tranquillity done large, as Nature herself alone could paint it.

Some paces along the western shore of the fiord was a manor-house, with its back set against the wild wood already mentioned. A most rural vegetative old manor-house, with an acre or two of black-and-white out-buildings attached to it, their thatched roofs all green and gold with lichens and moss. Here, anciently, the manorial retainers lived the life of a complete village; with the anvil here, the carpenter's shed there, the fishing-nets, stables, and all the rest of it closely contiguous. It is still a handsome old "desirable residence," though, from its

situation, a thought damp and secluded. Its two
tiers of windows, seven to each tier, stared blandly
at the impassive glistening waters of the fiord, and
its staircase gables at either side were, like the
extinguisher tower at one end, in excellent preserv-
ation. As for the red tiles on its roomy, deep-
descending roof, they had taken such a colour as
nothing less than a century of Jutland winters and
summers could give them. The style of the house
might be Christian the Fourthian, or a little earlier,
which is as much as to say Elizabethan in point of
time.

Returning to the pier, having had enough of the
fiord, I found that the jerseyed mariner had not
appealed to the Skive noses in vain. He had sold
his boxed dead fish, and was now triumphing with a
chest of shrimps, whose freshness was indicated in the
height they jumped. The buyers had hard work to
hold their purchases, which leapt to their very eye-
brows ere they consented to be tied up in pocket-
handkerchiefs or other portable prisons. One comely
young woman, with lustrous hair and limpid eyes,
filled her pockets with the live shrimps. But she was
evidently fresh from the baths, and in the humour
of an amphibian. The other dames held up their
hands at her, aghast before such unfeeling behaviour.

Skive's most winsome view-point, however, is its
church and cemetery which adjoin. They are

perched on the edge of a cliff, with a winding tributary of the Skive river in the lowlands beneath. Hence I saw a terrible number of square miles of dulness, though the naked land, with its modest colours, was rather soothing to the eye under the evening sunlight.

The church goes far back in the centuries. Its exterior is of the common kind, an unholy amalgam of granite and red brick, the former of cyclopean blocks. But inside it charms. Its nave is roofed by four shallow frescoed domes with stately groinings, and the altar end astonished by its soul-stirring gloom. There is an aisle to the south containing some pompous wooden funereal tablets, one in memory of a pastor of the seventeenth century, who died aged fifty-five, and left sixteen children to perpetuate his own mad philoprogenitiveness. The whole, with walls of vast thickness, even the partition walls having more than five feet of whitewashed granite in them.

There was a dead man in his coffin up by the altar, with candles set all round him, and the pews decorated with sprigs of yew for his burial service. I did not expect such treasure-trove, and in the inner dusk came upon the corpse only when I was against it. But the elderly woman with a broom who was preparing the church for the ceremonial told me he was a very harmless gentleman and much esteemed,

and that Skive would not soon see his like again—
mortuary sentiments that sounded familiar.

It was this same lady who insisted on my
scrutinizing carefully the crude pale pink frescoes
on the domes. Here was drama with a vengeance,
mostly on a Biblical or monkish foundation, but
such as could not have been so done with paint
brushes later than the Reformation period. I fancy
I made out a upas tree in one of the domes, an ugly
object with serpentine boughs and long thorns to
them, on which naked sinners were spiked mercilessly
through the middle. The old traditions and the
less old beliefs had somehow got blended in the
artist's mind, and had received priestly sanction
because of the spirit of their portrayal.

Skive's cemetery outside the church won esteem
for graces of a very different kind. Great part of it
was divided into so many little gardens with breast-
high hedges of box and thorn. The gardens were
full of flowers, or a tangle of roses and syringa. At
first sight the graves do not appear, but there they
are, disguised by the flowers. Few or no swollen
masses of marble or masonry. Generally just a square
foot of marble, with two clasped hands done on it in
relief, and the one word " Farewell," or a dove, a cross,
or the like emblem, with perhaps the affix of
" merchant," " baker," or " carpenter " to the dead
man's name. To most of the gardens there was a

seat, and in the trees overhead thrushes and black-
birds were carolling their thanks for the worms that
had come with the morning's rain.

I judge from the more elaborate epitaphs that they
do not live long in Skive. It is excusable. Life in
these little Jutland towns must be infinitely tedious;
not comparable, for comfort, to repose in so charming
a cemetery.

Supper at the Gluds Hotel was fully as solemn an
affair as the dinner that preceded it. It was vain to
try and inform my landlord that I would have liked
to sit with the ruck of travelling bagmen and others
who chanced to be lodging in his house. By the
names on the guest-board in the hall there must have
been at least twenty sojourners in the place, yet I saw
none of them. A huge room was devoted to me, and
the cook aided and abetted the head-waiter in looking
after me, with the landlord himself controlling all.

Already, in three days, it seemed to me that the
nights had shortened. Ten o'clock saw me again on
the church hill, whence the western sky shot crimson
ribbons of cloud almost to the zenith. The little
river in the lowlands mirrored these crimson ribbons.

On a bare space near the church there was one
of the most impoverished itinerant circuses I ever
beheld, with a mob of the Skive youth about it.
With others I bore a few minutes of the sport it
provided. There was, however, more outside in the

sighs and exclamations of the children whose circumstances saved them from disillusionment, and who
had a live piebald pony to feast their eyes on. With
the throng were four or five rather brazen young
women, who by twos found something to say to most
of the men in the throng. I was included with the
rest. This was at half-past ten, with very tolerable
daylight still about us. Really, I should not have
foretold such conduct in a place like Skive. It all
comes, I am afraid, from being in direct steamboat
communication with Copenhagen. And the dead
man lay in his coffin in the white-washed church,
with the spiked sinners on the dome overhead—not
one minute's walk from the piebald pony!

CHAPTER IV

The old capital of Jutland—Its churches, streets, smells, and
  present decay—King Eric Glipping the murdered—On
  wheels again—The Birgithe *kro*—A couple of bulls—
  The castle of Hald and its trivial history—Viborg's lake.

THERE was much rain in the night at Skive, and I
looked out on a lamentable sky when I drew up my
blind the better to drink my coffee at seven the next
morning. "Soft weather!" murmured the maidservant who brought me the breakfast while yet I
lay abed.

It was still "softer" afterwards. But my "Sunbeam" was mended, and awaited me at the railway
station, in charge of the hotel porter, who clearly
meant to hold it to ransom. Thither I went for it
in a preliminary drizzle. The river Skive, which I
crossed, had more water in it by much than eighteen
hours back.

As the roads and the clouds were all against
cycling, not to mention the wind, which hurried the
drizzle before it, I took train to Viborg, instead of
riding to that ancient place. The distance is

48

seventeen miles, and for a marvel we did it in an hour.

And now, for a change, I was to feast on mellowed buildings and monuments, instead of the bleak rusted moors. A thousand years ago the pagan gods were worshipped here as nowhere else in Jutland; and here the early kings of Denmark designed their little invasions and campaigns, whereby we suffered and others also. The old king Harald Blue Tooth was at Jellinge, by Veile, more than fifty miles away, superintending the setting up of the runic stone over the grave of his mother, Queen Thyra (it is still there), when a royal messenger approached him. The monarch, as was befitting, had the first word. "Have you ever seen anything so large as this stone carried off like this?" he inquired, with regal pride in his great tombstone. "Yes," answered the messenger; "yesterday, in the Viborg Thing (General Assembly), I saw thy son Sweyn carry off thy whole kingdom, which is certainly larger." It was in the year 1000 A.D., or thereabouts, that this same King Sweyn proceeded from his palace in Viborg, and, having joined fleets with his step-son the tributary king of Sweden, went against the doughty Olaf Tryggvason, slew him, and routed his ships, the consequence whereof was the annexation of Norway. Viborg was a proud city in those days, and had much to thank its heathen gods for.

E

But in A.D. 1895, alas! it seemed to me, at the outset, most remarkable for the foulness of its gutters. I gave one hand to my nose, while with the other I pushed my "Sunbeam" a little way up the nearest of its steep streets. Then I receded, and took up my abode in the Railway Hotel, close to the trains. It was a poor-looking inn, but at least gave me good chance of speedy flight if the weather and Viborg's smells together proved overwhelming.

The town stands on a very distinct hill, with a lake stretching north and south at its eastern side. It is a warm-looking association of tiled roofs and tree-tops, with the cathedral towers domineering all. As soon as I saw it, I felt that it was an ideal home for the stork: what with the foliage, the wide range of elevated spots for nests, and the lake with its shallows for the birds to dream themselves asleep, ankle deep, in; perhaps also its smells, which may be supposed appetizing to uncultured nostrils. And so it seemed, for I saw more storks there than elsewhere. I might further have taken it for a place of learning, by the multitude of small boys and girls with school books with whom I clashed as I climbed to the "Domkirk." The little girls pleased the eye in their blue pinafores, light pigtails, and useful clogs to keep them out of the filth that rotted in the gutters. The little boys were less smart, and their shouting in the quiet streets did not soothe the ear.

It was with a certain awe that I was glad to be conscious of that I came at length to the open space on which Viborg's cathedral is set. I rounded a corner and there it stood, the modern yet very old loadstone for Viborg's hopes and fears and aspirations. No pagan temple now, but on the site of one; its granite blocks placed one upon another fully eight hundred years ago; yet, thanks to recent fettling, as hale and fresh as if they were not six months from the quarry. Clearly a noble building, with no architectural flaw about it, and yet instantly recalling the Bloomsbury Chapel. But Viborg's "Domkirk" is an original piece of Norman work—the diamond on which so much paste brilliancy has been modelled. Denmark's Parliament and the nation did well, a decade or two back, to make the restoration of this church a personal and State necessity. It was taken to pieces stone by stone, and reared up again with such care and art that little has been disarranged, though all rottenness has been removed from it. If ever a church was good for a millennium straight off, this "Domkirk" of Viborg now is. Perhaps its spotless granite, methodical windows, and precise campaniles (two pairs of these, though with bells in but one of the towers) would look better down by the Adriatic, under a blue sky in keeping with such pureness and regularity. But one must take things as they are, and Viborg may be cordially congratulated on a priceless possession, whether its skies are cloudless or grey as the North Sea vapours can breed them. It may seem odd to mention in one breath the Bloomsbury Chapel off Oxford Street, and the Basilica of Aquileia, between the Eastern Alps and the Adriatic; nevertheless, both of them are kindred to Viborg's cathedral. The latter is own brother to it, or at least a first cousin. But the bar-sinister, very sinister, lies across the other relationship.

They could not open the "Domkirk" to visitors until eleven o'clock this day, because the pastor was holding a confirmation class in it. I filled the intervening hour at the only other church of consequence in the town, the south parish church, or, as it was called centuries ago, the Blackfriars Church. My devious approach to it was by Greyfriars Street. There is not much appearance of the mediæval about Viborg; the numerous conflagrations have taken care of that; one must therefore be thankful for the flavour discoverable in its nomenclature.

Here was a contrast indeed with the cold classicism of the "Domkirk." Instead of granite, red brick; instead of towers, a façade of the staircase order; instead of standing as unguardedly in its square as a lamp-post, graves and grass hedged it about, and venerable trees shedding rain-drops upon mossy tombs.

The church was built in the thirteenth century, and was burned down, with almost all Viborg, in 1726. As one sees it now, therefore, it is but a rough copy of its early self, with, however, presumably, its old loftiness of roof, which makes it imposing. In shape a Latin cross, with domed ceilings and the iniquity of whitewash everywhere inside, save on the pews, the panelling, and the pavement. But for liveliness of colour commend me to its great organ in the west, where blues and reds and yellows and greens do their utmost to frighten the whitewash out of countenance. The pews and panels are as interesting as a peep-show at a fair. The door to each pew and each panel has a painting on it, allegorical, whimsical, or purely imaginative, with a text or inscription thereto. Thus to the words " Our life is a vapour," you have the picture of a bewildered man under a tree, holding out his hand towards a fleeing mist ; to the passage from Job, "I said to the worm, My mother and my sister," two skulls with vipers crawling from their various cavities and wriggling consumedly. One picture in about three has a skeleton in it; the artists seem to have tried their very hardest to be grisly. But conceive how these hundreds of decorations (for the church is more than 200 feet long) must impress the infant minds brought up in it. It depends, of course, entirely upon the child whether the show proves a curse or an inspiration. For my part, I should dearly have liked to do my early church-going in this most thrilling of Biblical picture-galleries.

I was intent upon a smiling skeleton, with a spade in one hand and a bunch of flowers in the other, when a bevy of young women bounced into the church, chattering and laughing fit to convulse a Scotch elder. They raced up the aisle to the altar and back again. It must have been a challenge; if so, the one with the poppy in her hat won it. Then they espied me by the panel, and laughed and talked the more. All the time I was in the place they made their gay noises: whether I was far from them examining the excellent coloured metal altar-piece (a fifteenth-century achievement), including Simeon in the temple with large spectacles on his nose, and the four cover paintings, which seem meritorious enough for a museum of arts; or whether I was close to them, and therefore, one would suppose, a tacit reproach, even if not a source of maidenly embarrassment. I left them giggling among these painted aids to holiness, and know not to this day what their purpose was: a baptism, a churching, or a burial.

In the "Domkirk," on the other hand, all was peaceful and solid, and eloquent of the united perfection of taste exercised by a nation upon a national treasure. No fripperies, unless the boards

with the five hymn-numbers hung to the columns
on either side the aisle could be so regarded. The
pews would be better away, but this is the only
suggestion that I would offer to the Bishop in his
palace to the east of the church. It is a majestic
temple, unmistakably Protestant, in spite of the
large crucifix on the wall by the central dome, with
room in it for the soul's breathings, and much solemn
beauty in the mosaic of its apse to tone down the
awe of its stern cold granite arches and columns,
arch upon arch, to the narrow windows above the
triforium close upon the painted wagon roof, as spick
and span as the furniture in an upholsterer's shop.

My guide was scarcely the conventional cicerone.
Viborg is not in the highway of tourists. He did
not, therefore, make as much of the scraps of the
murdered King Eric Glipping's body as he might
have done; and, having led me to the choir steps,
he left me to exult as I pleased in the prospect.
I liked the shapely grey granite pulpit on its three
columns of red granite, in their turn supported on
the backs of three granite lions. An old hour-glass
was on the pulpit ledge, still used as when the great
seven-armed candelabrum was brought from Lübeck
just four centuries ago. This object is nine feet
high, and, like the pulpit, rests on lions. Its fat
candles might of themselves almost illumine the
whole church.

Marsk Stig and his colleagues in conspiracy murdered King Eric Glipping at Finderup, a mile or two distant, in 1286. Hither the dead king was brought and entombed in the choir, where he stayed until the conflagration of 1726, which left of him only the morsels of skin and charred hair now on view. But from the time of his interment until 1774, Viborg bore him in mind; twelve school-boys chanting every morning the " Vaadesangen," or " song of woe," in the crypt under his tomb. To this crypt my guide led me with the facile phrase, " The best thing in the Domkirk." As a crypt, it is as impressive as it can be, and completely preserved, so that if the first twelve choristers who dirged for King Eric could be brought back to it, they would find it as they left it. The crypt is the only part of the " Domkirk" that needed no restoration, and its tiled floor and Norman pillars of granite and porphyry would bear the full daylight as well as the furbished aisle and chancel overhead.

The old chapels of the cathedral, anciently dedicated to Roman saints, are now little but sepulchral chambers. Into one of them, in 1150, the famous cleric Kjeld, who had done much for Viborg, had himself carried on a bier when he was at the last gasp. Others joined St. Kjeld (for he was canonized), and chief of them Bishop Gunner, who died in his hundred and first year, and of whom

we are told that, though the most hospitable of
men, he himself drank nothing but Danish mead.
The Krag family have a snug chapel near the west
door, with five great decorated coffins in it, and a
beautiful wrought-iron wicket of the seventeenth
century. Elsewhere many other coffins appeared,
each large enough for a family—monstrous vain
things in their faded velvets, tarnished angels set
at the corners, shields, coats-of-arms, and verbose
inscriptions. To get the savour of their dust and
futile pomp out of my mouth, I climbed to the bell
tower, where the wind was vigorous and sweet, and I
felt the last rain-drops of the day. The sky was
blue over Viborg, and its lake was an azure pool
with green park-lands on its other side. I was here
some four hundred feet above the water, and could
see where the Viborgers, twenty years after Eric
Glipping's assassination, got hold of Aage Kagge,
one of Marsk Stig's confederates in the deed, and
slew him and his men, afterwards casting their
bodies on the slopes for the ravens to eat. I wonder
if the storks had then domesticated themselves in
Jutland, and if they too, being tempted, would
have declined to sup on a perjured traitor and his
men.

Our Danish cousins of Viborg in the middle ages
were just as rough and wild as ourselves in those
days, and fully as religious. The town at one time

had twelve churches, and six monasteries and convents. Perhaps the nuns in these last were now and then insubordinate and frivolous. Even the repressive north could not wholly subdue the molecules in their blood. But nothing could excuse the immurement of one of the poor ladies in a convent wall. In 1799, the skeleton of a woman was found bricked up where the nunnery of St. Budolph had been. There is no record of her or her crime.

Viborg saw kings and bishops and cardinals enough in its palmy centuries. It also then had an annual fair, or *snapsthing*, of sixteen days' duration, famous all over the north. They came hither from Italy, and of course Englishmen, Germans, and Dutchmen pressed their wares into it. The New Square in the middle of the town was its site, and so great was the demand for accommodation round the square, that the burghers and others paid their rent for the year by letting their houses in whole or part during this lively fortnight. The Cathedral started the fair with a solemn ringing of its bell at about half-past ten in the morning of June the thirteenth, and closed the fair on the twenty-ninth in the same way. We are told of the jugglers and jesters and merchants who then glorified Viborg; of the demand for honey cakes at one particular booth, and the pretty Dutch girls who elsewhere dispensed sweet wafer biscuits. But, like other fairs, this of Viborg lost its character, and latterly became dissolute. In the eighteenth century, although the royal band came to increase its seductions, the curse of gaming helped it to an end. They gambled in the streets, and in the clubs there was so much faro and basset, and to such a tune, that "not seldom the unfortunate gamester drowned his body in the lake." All which was deplorable enough, but quite in keeping with the progress of civilization in other European towns better known than this little capital of Jutland.

My Danish friend, on the steamer and afterwards, had given as one reason for her love of England, that there you are unnoticed—"There are so many people that they do not recognize a stranger." In Viborg I found it much otherwise. Jutland's capital paid me the homage of considerable attention as I strolled about its odoriferous thoroughfares: St. Mogen's Street, St. Hans' Street, the Great Dump and the Little Dump (*dump* being Danish for "slope"), trying to transfigure it into a semblance of its well-burnt-out past. But this effort of imagination was too severe to keep up, and there was so little to aid me. A few low-browed half timber houses with carved beams were all the relics I could see, though the illusion of diamond panes to the windows and the deceptive overcoating of whitewash made many

of the streets look downright ancient. The town is
still a garrison depôt. I saw some of the soldiers
being exercised. They had not yet learnt to keep
their thumbs tucked in, nor to keep their countenances either. Their age too was, on the average,
about midway in the teens, and their height was
very moderate. Hence I put them down as recruits.
I do not think our youngest regiments would have
much to fear from these soldiers of good King
Christian. Honest lads they probably were, but
more likely to be appreciated by their mothers and
lady cousins than the drill-sergeants who had them
in charge.

When I had spent a long morning in Viborg, and
dined off an inimitable arrangement of cold slices
set round a gigantic lobster, itself decorated with
pretty garden stuff, I hied me to my hotel and
called for my "Sunbeam." The ostler was at the
moment hissing over it as if it had been a hard-
skinned horse. He had polished it radiantly, having
been bidden by his master. And then I mounted
and rode to the south by the road that is a continuation of Little St. Michael Street, where the Little
Dump joins into it. I was for Hald, which every
Jutlander who loves beautiful scenery will tell you
is a vision of romantic loveliness. You see, here in
Viborg I was in the heart of Jutland, far out of reach
of the saltness in the North Sea's winds, and there-

fore with no excuse for barrenness. I confess I was curious about Hald, which appears a good deal in the Sagas. I was also eager to see if the three crowns (3s. 4½d.) they had charged me at Skive for repairs had been well invested.

The road was fair, and the wind, being west, did not hinder this brief run to the south. I soon crossed the railway, and looked up to the right at Finderup, where they murdered King Eric Glipping. It seemed to have little except a church to its name. Then I came of a sudden to the beginning of the wood of Hald, here a bright reach of planted moorland, with yellow larches among the purple heather, and a well-flogged broad track through it. A troop of warriors were before me, marching as if they had had much recent practice, and an officer on a cycle, who minded the ruts less than I did.

Annually, Denmark's soldiers camp on this moor for their manœuvres. These were just at an end, and the troop ahead of me was the rearguard of the batch. I could have envied the men their exercise and life in such a spot.

But I soon saw that I was astray, and had to return to the main Aarhus road, which I had left; and then, for four miles or so, I careered between pretty oak woods in a sweet scent of bark. Dark juniper in clumps graced the undergrowth, and moss in profusion. That there was game in the wood I learnt from the prohibitive boards on the trees— a few deer and some pigeons, I believe; little else.

I rode on in the gallant sunshine and breeze till I came to a fairy little dell with a rushing green river in it, and a mill. Also a *kro*, that of Birgithe, with the heathery hills rising almost loftily in a long ridge behind. In Denmark there are about three kinds of houses for the entertainment of travellers. First, the hotel, a building confined to towns; second, the *gicstgivergaard*, or inn, in which the stranger is fed and lodged somewhat roughly, but still suffici- ently well; third, the *kro*, or public-house, where you may always drink something, but in which you cannot always rely upon a bed. The Birgithe house belonged to the third category. An aged country- man was sunning his stubbly beard outside it, while he smoked a great pipe with a Venus head on its bowl.

"Where," I inquired, "is the lake of Hald, and its famous castle?"

But the rustic found my accent awkward, and not until he had put both hands to his ears did he catch my meaning. Then, instead of replying, he questioned me.

"Of what nation are you?"

"An Englishman," quoth I, mindful that, accord- ing to local tradition, it was at Viborg or Hald that Prince Hamlet slew his mother and stepfather, and

divers others who interfered with his scheme of
things, and hoping that the countryman's education
had taught him the word Shakespeare.

The next instant he ran indoors, and bellowed the
news, and out came a smiling though nervous landlady and a stout landlord. Ere I understood what
was happening, I was whisked into the state apartment, and coffee and cakes were before me. Both
my entertainers tried their hardest to get some
informing conversation with me; but the task was
too laborious to be protracted, and so I was left to
my refreshment and the four cigars I had chosen at
a venture from a box. I spent a gentle half-hour
thus taking my ease. Once I heard something
amusing. The countryman had secured a comrade
outside, and was telling him what the *kro* held in
its best room.

"Come in and see him," he urged.

"*Nei*," said the other hesitantly.

"For company's sake."

"*Nei*."

"Come, now."

"*Nei*, I will not;" and off he went.

Nei means "no," as any one may suppose. But
the emphasis this Jutlander put into the word made
it latterly into the most petrifying of negatives.
He ought to have eviscerated me of all my self-
esteem.

Fourpence half-penny was all that I paid for the sport the Birgithe *kro* gave me.

Then I sought Hald's lake afresh. I was close to it, but woodlands and hills stood between us, and deep rivulets and very wet meadows studded with flowers. For a good hour I lost myself in these lonely environs of the lake; pushed my cycle through tangled brakes, over rotten trees, and down fearsome slopes matted with heather and tall scrub. Then I harked back, and tried another way. This time I came upon a couple of irate bulls, mercifully tethered, though close to the sandy rut that was all my track to the water. The way they pawed the ground at me, with their heads low and sonorous mutterings in their throats, was not encouraging, especially as I knew not the length of their chains. I was glad when I had done with them, with not a yard to spare, and was again breasting the wood, through sand more than ankle deep.

Thus at last I broke on to high land free from trees, and looked forward at the blue lake in its hollow, with its shores partly wooded, part velvety green grass, and part brown moorland, some two hundred feet above it. It was here I passed a couple of abandoned wells, and some fragments of red-brick masonry; all that remains of Brattingsborg, or the fort built by King Valdemar the Third to overawe that famous Jutland nobleman, Niels Bugge, who then held the castle of Hald in the hollow by the lake side, less than a mile away. Other reason for a fort here there could be none, and so in the five centuries since then "Valdemar's skansen" has slowly but certainly drifted into nothingness.

Niels Bugge was a worthy warrior, and thought himself nearly the equal of his king. When Valdemar pressed him with bribes to surrender the castle, he replied—

"I will not break my plight for gold,
What I have sworn to that I'll hold."

He had much more to say to his sovereign in defiance, who then set about his *skansen*, quietly reproving Niels for his talkativeness:

"My dear lord Bugge, make not such a quacking,
For I come not yet to send you packing."

Eventually the stout baron was murdered by some fisherman of the Little Belt, when he was returning from a fruitless visit to the king, to request that an end might be put to the siege. As the way was in those days, the monarch then, though mightily relieved, turned upon the assassins who had done him such service, "the Middle Part men, Christ give them sorrow"; and for many years their town was condemned to pay an annual sum as blood-money. His majesty thus profited all ways—possessed the castle, was rid of a turbulent, daring lord, was spared the

F

expense of a further siege (then in its fourth year), and put silver into his regal pocket.

From the *skansen* I scrambled toilsomely to the water-side, having to lift my "Sunbeam" over several gates, and thus came to the red ruins of the old citadel. A young officer was sitting pensively on the keep. He and I had the place to ourselves, and the cuckoo, with its broken note (it was June the eighteenth), alone vexed our day-dreams.

The romance of Hald must be sought in books. There is no one here to tell you anything, and only the feeble pile of dislodged and parting bricks, the clover-sweet grass, the blue water, the woods, and the stern, bare moor beyond, to make a setting for the tales told by tradition.

A tranquil, pretty spot, but nothing to Esthwaite Water in Lancashire, which is reckoned one of the inferior of our English lakes.

I rode back from Hald by the modern manor-house (worth many castles), and after one disconcerting capsize into a ditch—due to thinking of other things—reached Viborg in time for supper. The cathedral from the Aarhus road has a fine commanding air, with the houses scarcely knee-deep about it.

There were eight or nine of us at the *table d'hôte*, seven at least being regular guests. Among them were two young officers, who gave us pipeclay bows, but were above passing the salt to their lady neighbours. I am afraid it was not a very genteel hotel, for the young lady next to me seemed unnerved when I paid her any civility, though her mother— a rotund person with easy smiles—nudged her to accept all of that coin she could obtain. But the stewed eels were excellent.

The night being at hand, I had no intention of making a cruise when I strolled out afterwards with my cigar to take a final view of Viborg, the great but fallen. I chanced upon the lake by hazard, led thither by the stream of people, enjoying the cool evening air with the gusto of Neapolitans. Then I espied three of my dear friends the storks, standing well from the shore in shallow water. It was now short work to hire a boat from the dilapidated old man who had them in his keeping. His charge was twopence the hour.

I have seldom got more for my twopence. To begin with, it was a very strange boat, and the water gurgled into it freely from a hole. Then I grounded when I was near the storks, who paid me the compliment of complete indifference. By no vocal entreaty could I stir the birds, though their affectation of slumber in such an attitude was a hollow fraud. In these shallows I soon realized that I was hard upon some of Viborg's main sewers. But it was not without difficulty that I removed myself.

Thence I rowed to the south end of the lake, and fell in with a fisherman who had caught nothing and was in a loquacious mood. He began chattering at a great rate, much too fast for me; his speed gradually diminished; my remarks puzzled him, and finally he decided that he would have more chance of a fish somewhere else.

At half-past ten I was still on the lake, with pools of golden light from the golden sky about my boat. But when the "Domkirk" clock struck the half-hour I rowed to shore, astounded the boatman by giving him threepence, and so home to bed.

CHAPTER V

Bad cycling weather—A climb to the uplands—Aalstrup—
Gjedsted—Royal going—Björnsholm Kloster—Ranum—
Lögstör—Aggersund in the rain—A lukewarm reception
—Aggersborg.

YET another inauspicious morning. There had
been a halo about the sun at Hald in the beginning
of the evening, and the halo proved to have signifi-
cance. About half a cyclone was blowing when I
breakfasted in my Viborg inn, and rain was at hand.

Still, weather good or weather menacing, I had
had enough of Jutland's metropolis. I was for
Lögstör, where the shore of the Aalborg Amt almost
kisses the shore north of the Lim Fiord, and where
I hoped to get ferried across the Aggersund. It
seemed well to get a little way on the road by rail,
considering the portents. Therefore, "Sunbeam"
and I took tickets for Aalstrup.

It was a tempestuous little journey, and of
incredible steepness for Jutland. In eleven miles
we must have risen four hundred feet. The engine
fussed over it, and now and then paused as if to

69

glance backwards and say, " Only think what a feat
I have achieved !" When we had been moving for
fifty minutes, we had gone eleven miles.

And how it blew all the time, with inky black
clouds over the dun moors ! The carriage rattled
in the blasts. At the railway stations the ladies
clutched their skirts, pale-faced with alarm. They
had already tied black ribbons over their headgear
and under their chins. A certain sedate spaniel,
sitting full in the wind current at Skals, had its
spacious ears flapped to and fro with an energy that
must have warmed its temples; and a melancholy
hen that ventured on the platform was hustled past
the flapping spaniel with its tall feathers over its
head, and cries of terror that made the dog start. At
these upland stations the red-coated postal authorities
made bright spots. It is their high office to take
and tender the day's letter-bag, and, pending the
train's arrival, to be sociable with the pig-tailed
damsels who happen to be going a journey.

I was getting to a land thickly pimpled with the
graves of ancient Danes. On one ridge there were
seven of the mounds cheek by jowl with each other.
And yet the district seemed as little favourable to a
dense population of great men as any could be. The
moorland slopes stretched dismally on either hand,
up or down; pale yellow for the most part with
sickly grass, but with vivid green oases where a

meadow or an acre of wind-blown barley had been prepared. Bars of black peat stood in the hollows, and every mile or so there was a stumpy farmstead of red brick with a roof of grey thatch. Under proper atmospheric conditions, such landscapes might be picturesque to the passing traveller not doomed to dwell in their midst. But I beheld them all under a gloom that was Satanic.

At Aalstrup the railway could go no higher without climbing into the clouds. Here the wind-claps shook the station, and rain was falling. But I was not going to give in and condemn myself to a dreary morning at the Aalstrup inn. With such a breeze at my back, or nearly, I hoped for good progress, and I would take my chance of a soaking ere I got to Gjedsted, four miles or so due west, where I designed to dine.

It was a rough-and-tumble road, and I was soon soaked by the rain. But in rather less than twenty minutes I reached Gjedsted village, having been accompanied all the way by a brace of swallows, whose flashes across my leading wheel were about as closely judged as they could have been. It was an ugly district, but at Gjedsted I espied some stately houses, well-grown trees, and the misty waters of one of the broads alongside which, more or less, I hoped to run after dinner right away to Lögstör.

The Gjedsted inn was not a polished establishment.

They did not seem to care for a guest, and made no offer of dry clothes. But little by little the landlord thawed into moderate amiability, and in the end I was allowed to sit with him and a very burly fish merchant, and take my share of the dinner. His wife waited on us. We were expected to assail the dishes with our forks as the mood took us, a pastime at which the fish merchant excelled. There was a large wood-cut of Ibsen in the room, and yet they could not understand where came in the pleasure of cycling about a strange country with no ulterior motive, such as butter, beasts, or hay. However, they agreed cheerfully that I was free to kill or weary myself in the way most congenial to me. Our clinking of glasses after the cloying, ill-cooked meal removed the last shred of positive antipathy between us. It was the good *aqua vita* of Aalborg, not excelled in Denmark.

After two hours, with a clearer sky, though as vigorous a wind as ever, I sought my cycle in the inn stables. The dear thing was surrounded by the Gjedsted villagers, the village blacksmith apparently using it as a text for a professional oration. This blacksmith seemed glad to see me, and as well as I could make out from his brogue (they talk abomin- able Danish in some parts of Jutland), he bade the others follow my movements closely in mounting and working the pedals, and see if he were not perfectly right in his assertions. We capped earnestly, all the crowd of us, and then I did my best to satisfy the blacksmith.

I was now in for a triumphant progress to the north. The wind was right in the small of my back, and the rather sandy road had positively benefited by the rain. No sooner was I in the saddle than I was out of Gjedsted, conscious of having impressed that sluggish small hamlet. My "Sunbeam" took unto itself wings, and without effort I flew. Some dogs chased me from the village with imperative cries, but they soon had enough of it, and I was again in the wilds, with moor on either hand, larks singing above me, a sweet invigorating air to breathe, and two or three white churches with red saddles decorating the bleakness before me. The crunching of my "Sunbeam's" tyres on the fine shellac substance of the road was music as blithe as the trilling of the larks.

But at the first of the churches I was caught by a squall, and trundled briskly to the lee side of it. The parsonage was near, and no other building. Had I known the pastor was at home I would have thrown myself on his hands, for the Danish priest is, as a rule, a kindly cultured soul. But I shrank from entreating courtesies from his wife, possibly alone in the house.

Fovlum church has some granite columns to its

porch that are an indisputable certificate of its age. I traced a lion's head on one, and a rude man, legs and all, on either side of the lion.   But the winds and rain had flattened the sculptures.   Its bayed apse was also comely.   The entire building was of granite blocks, scarcely less old than Viborg's cathedral.

Under blue sky again and a renewal of the breeze I pushed on famously, passed through a degraded village called Stistrup, with boats drawn ashore from the Rüggaarde Broad, which touches it, and many tatterdemalion children, who fled with screams before my bell signal.   The villagers came forth from their hovels with one accord and watched my flight.   A poverty-stricken community, like none others I had seen in Jutland.

My next pause was at Strandby, with a church and a mill ; the former large, of granite, and in the pangs of restoration.   Old oaken beams, sculptured capitals, and mortuary stones lay about in disarray, and the wind howled in the tower, up which I climbed to look across the now blue water at Fuurland, a small island at the head of the Salling peninsula.   But there are no hills on Fuurland to give it individuality, and the strait between it and the mainland does but just exist.

From Strandby I ran six miles without halt to Björnsholm Kloster, crossing the river Trend, and seeing hardly a soul.   A loose drove of thirsty cows blocked the way near the disestablished monastery, and when I had compassed the tired beasts I was free to rest among the graves and elder bushes of this pretty wooded nook, with the long white body of the church between me and the wind. The sun burned here. I felt as if I had ridden all the way to the Riviera, and had the right to look for aloes and orange trees in the cloister gardens.

The monastery has gone as a whole, but its out-line remains. They have turned its precincts into a modern cemetery. Graves are dug in the old residential parts of the building. On one mound were recent tributes of affection, the ribbons to the wreaths none the worse for the rain, and at the grave-side the granite base of a massive column cropped out. Capitals with ornate beading were discoverable among the grass. A serpent's head cunningly done in the stone also caught the eye. Farther afield was half-an-acre or so of red-brick *débris*, with vegetation thick about it, and a copse of trees on a knoll above, all the trees with their boughs bent hard to the east. In its day this monastery of Björnsholm must have been highly important; the hoarse cuckoo in its woods now gave out a note as pathetic as its fortunes. I could not gain access to the church. But a shocking charnel-house beneath it was open to the winds, and showed a depressing medley of broken coffins a hundred or

two years old, with their bony tenants lolling forth
as if they had been prematurely entombed and had
died in the act of struggling for freedom. Adjoining
the red-tiled church (whose colour harmonized well
with the now radiant blue sky) was a great barrack
of a building, with piles of domestic rubbish behind
it, and many windows not all filled with glass. The
building had inmates, for I could hear them brawling. And that is all I know about it. The *kloster*
may be a madhouse or a union: its appearance
qualifies it for either calling.

Hence, with a mutter of thunder behind me, I
flashed to Ranum before a strong long gust of wind.
The rain was beginning when I came to the Ranum
inn, where I drank coffee in a very prim guest-room,
and enjoyed the society of the innkeeper's son, who
was good enough to compliment me on my Danish.
"You might be a fellow-countryman," he said at
length, which spoiled all. Flattery is an art; too
much and too little of it are alike worse than none
at all.

The shower kept me dallying at Ranum, but the
moment the sun peeped out on the wet roofs I
moved forward. Malle church was left on one side,
with a curious serpentine ridge of viking tombs;
and thence I ran to Lögsted, as if Boreas himself
were puffing at my shoulder-blades. The church
here resembled the other granite churches I had

seen during the day: whitewash was its chief attribute, after its situation on the summit of a considerable watershed of moor. And now Lögstör was in sight, with a fine new steeple, and the masts of small ships among its houses. My course was downhill to it, and I was soon there.

A bright red and green and white new little town is Lögstör, well paved at the west entrance to the Aggersund, that is to say, on the waterway between the North Sea and the Cattegat. The Lögstör Broad is the most extensive of the salt pools of this ramified inland sea. Low islets clasped by sandbanks and mud are plentiful north of the town, so that the passing steamers have to feel their way east or west somewhat carefully.

A certain neat hotel, with a row of green shutters to its bedrooms, almost seduced me into a sojourn at Lögstör. But the town contains really nothing of interest: it is too new for that. Its port dues and sand-dredgers did not appeal to me.

The ferry was my bourne. To come at it I had nearly three miles more to run, parallel with the water, along a nicely-curved shore line. And how it did rain during the quarter of an hour of that run! Right glad was I to flee into the ferry shelter on the water's edge, and wait there until the ferryman returned from the north shore. The Sound here cannot be much more than the sixth of a mile across:

the steamship *Udvalla*, which glided past in the rain, looked as if a light turn of the helm would run her in a moment or two on either shore.

The ferryman might have stood for the model of an ancient Norseman, so massive of build was he, so lustily bearded, and with such a calm, clear, steady gaze in his blue eyes. His opinion of the wind was that it might shift in the night, and of the Aggersund inn, that they would have room for me. He lifted my cycle in and out as if it had been a child's bauble, yet with its five-sided portmanteau it weighed something well over thirty-five pounds.

The time was now six o'clock, and I was content to take mine ease in a hostelry. But they did not show any enthusiasm about me at the Aggersund inn.

I wished the pretty girl of the house a "goodevening," and asked her if I could sleep there.

"Yes," she said, and resumed her knitting. Her little yellow-haired sister, however, warmed me with a smile.

"Also I am hungry. Can I eat something?"

"Perhaps so. I will ask," replied the girl.

But she did not ask, nor even look at me; she only worked her needles. And she did not blush or show any sign of confusion that might excuse such apparent inhospitality towards a very wet stranger.

"Well," said I, "be so kind as to show me my room."

Instead of complying, the damsel gathered up her little yellow-haired sister, and without a word departed from the coffee-room, leaving me humbled.

The rural Danes take some comprehending. I thought so the more when this girl's large mother appeared, and also seemed indifferent about my comfort. She laughed at my wetness, but showed me an attic. Later they served me an omelette and a beefsteak, and the spoons and forks were of old silver. And little by little the haughty girl of the inn thawed, so that ere the meal was over, of her own accord she marched into my room with the youngest born of the house in her arms, sat where I could see her best, and asked me questions. She had blue eyes and freckles, and a wonderful little figure. But her self-possession was the most remarkable thing of all about her; she interrogated me with the business-like air of a Civil Service examiner. And afterwards she yawned very wide, showing unblemished white little teeth, and shaking the baby, began to croon to it, so that I could there and then have taken her in my arms for her beautiful motherliness.

"I am inclined to stop here two nights," I said, having briefly outlined my plans for the morrow.

"So!" said she. "Then I will kill a pigeon for

your dinner to-morrow, and there are ripe currants in the garden."

I did stop at Aggersund two nights. But the day between them was not, as you might suppose, devoted to idling and conversational practice with this pretty girl. Very far otherwise. Nor was this evening either.

At half-past eight I left the inn to walk to the old-time royal residence of Aggersborg, a mile away, and idiotically contrived to make a five-mile business of it ere I was back at Aggersund.

The road carried me too far inland, towards one of the most assuming hill pimples I had yet seen. A wooden-shoed peasant whom I questioned about the mound said that a king lay under it. And even while he said so two lively urchins leaped upon it, and played in the strong glow of the western sky. When they came off it others followed, little girls with swinging hair-tails among them. There was a school-house in the neighbourhood, and the youngsters had only been let loose at that hour of the night. What, I wonder, would our own children think if we used the long summer days mainly as a pretext for extending their school-time?

A bracing, unpicturesque land this corner of the Thisted Amt proved to be until I came to Aggersborg, with potatoes and barley about the houses, but more heath and pasture than arable land. The kine were chained, and the sheep tethered in couples; in the latter case often a ewe with her own lamb, both striving hard to get as far as possible from each other, and fighting between-times. The social instinct may be strong in the lower animals, as with us; but they, as little as we, like to have it unduly insisted on.

When I reached Aggersborg it was past ten o'clock, and I expected to find a slumberous tranquillity over the village. No such thing, though. Two leathery dames were gossiping in the churchyard, with milk in pails by their feet; and in the gardens, men, women, and children were weeding industriously. A cuckoo and several larks also kept up the illusion of broad daylight, which was scarcely belied by the misty crimson in the western sky over the water, and the islets that line the shore, and are only parted from the mainland when the tide is up.

Once upon a time the king had his palace in Aggersborg. I saw the place thereof: a desolate heap of earth, girt round with tall nettles and borage. For all I know, or for all any one here with whom I spoke could tell me, the king himself moulders in peace under the mound whereon the children play before and after school hours.

Modern Aggersborg is a collection of graceful cottages embowered in trees, and other cottages much less graceful. When the west wind has a boisterous fit on, they must want all the protection against it that they can get here.

It was late when I returned to Aggersund. But though late, a travelling bagman had only just arrived in his vehicle and pair, and was watching the removal of his samples while he smoked a thoughtful pipe. Somewhat later he and I were put to bed in the attic, with a very thin partition of laths between us. The man might have been a merchant in snores from the variety he played upon the circumambient air during the two hours I perforce lay awake criticizing them.

CHAPTER VI

Blue skies and a moderate breeze—A dairy district—Aagaard—
Fjerridslev — The church of Kollerup—Hjortels—The
Bay of Lamentations—Glorious sands and waves—A
weary time on the moors—Farm hospitality—Tired out.

MY comrade the bagman appeared the next
morning while I was drinking coffee with the yolks
of two eggs in it. By the half-circles under his
eyes, his noises in the night had rested him as
little as they had soothed me. We gave each
other "good-day," and then, to my audience, he
dropped a series of acid remarks about the people
and the wayfaring accommodation of our part of
Denmark. "We're rats, or it looks like it, or
why should they put us in such holes to sleep!"
"And the stuff they call cognac here! Why, my
good sir, it's as sugary as Chartreuse. My stomach
paid in the night for the drop I had before retiring!"
"Talk about manners, too. Oh, my heart!"

The gentleman was a German, and slipped this
leash of censures in his own tongue. But the
instant the damsel with the freckles entered he

83

bloomed with bows and smiles. I was glad to see she stared at him as icily as she had stared at me. Perhaps her womanly intuition told her what a perjured traitor to his own sentiments the man was; for he ordered a glass of the bad cognac forthwith, and then proceeded to light a pipe and burrow among his invoices and address books.

It was the serenest morning I had experienced in Jutland; quite in keeping with its crimson promise at 2 a.m., when the bagman's music held me sleepless, and I had seen the day rise new-born across the opaline waters of the Sound. The sky was all blue and it was very warm.

I told my landlady I might not be back until eight in the evening. That meant a ten hours' absence, which she seemed to think called for an explanation. I mentioned Svinklöv and other names.

"Did I," she retorted, "expect to reach these places on my cycle?"

"Such a hope was not unreasonable," I said.

"You will see, my God," she exclaimed heartily; and then, with a quaint, serious change of countenance, she wished me a pleasant journey, adding as an afterthought, that such contrivances as my cycle were perhaps well suited to towns like Copenhagen, or even Aalborg, but that I had made a mistake to think to travel in comfort on it in her part of the province.

"You shall learn for yourself," she wound up with, "and the pigeon will be cooked for eight."

This Cassandra-like note disturbed me, and for a while I smoked among the currant bushes in the small inn garden and pondered her words. But I decided to have my own way. Experience by hearsay is never worth much, and the main road through the village (a continuation of that from Lögstör, broken by the waters of the Sound) ran so very straight to the north, without apparent deterioration for miles. The larks, too, were chanting gaily, and I itched to be off.

The stable of the Aggersund inn stands rather more publicly towards the road than the inn itself— a roofed shed, open at both ends. But no one commits theft in Jutland. So said the ostler when he prepared my "Sunbeam" for its day's adventures, having postponed attention to the bagman's shay, with its green plush cushions and heavy woodwork. I bought Virginia tobacco in the store next the inn at a penny the ounce, and then mounted and rode to the north. A wind had come up and blew in my face, but it was not too strong, and the gradient of the road, though upward, was not too steep.

Earlier in the morning I had noticed an unusual company of milk-cans in carts making for the south from the north. I now met more of them, and cattle in droves. This argued a rich pastoral country, though for a few miles the land seemed of the ordinary impoverished kind, with pools among the heather and wavy ridges of moor, as untouched by the hand of man as at the first settling of Jutland, save for the rearing of gravel in burial heaps. But I learnt something about the cows when I came to Aagaard, or the River Manor-house.

This fine old property of woods, and meadows enclosed among its woods, with a river making a moat round it, is devoted to milk and butter. Many other manor-houses in Jutland have the same aims. Either their latter-day owners are shrewd farmers instead of barons, or else the aristocrats are trying to make money like the farmers.

I approached the manor-house by a miry lane, trampled by cow-heels, with the richest imaginable meadows on either side, pressed by tall trees. To the left stood the ancient building — low, with clean, yellow-washed walls, massive as a citadel, and with tokens of wealth and refinement in the draping of its windows and its gardens. But to the right were other buildings, acres of them, also clean and trim; the stalls for the kine, sheds for milk-cans, and dairies. The sunlight gleamed on many a metal *amphora*, and the voices of milkmaids could be heard singing. A handsome clock in a tower made one think of the rigid precision of our home factory life, and of the contrast between that and this. And now from one of the yards out trooped scores of comely milking cows, long-backed, plump, and with lazy swing of the feet, though with tails vigorously warring against the flies. The bright-coloured old house, as fresh as paint in spite of its age, the cool green of its many trees, its grass, the clear rushing stream, the dragon-flies speeding across the meadows and athwart the water, and the rare blue sky above this sequestered, shadowed nook, made up a comforting picture of rural life in Jutland at its best. Yet outside the domain of Aagaard, in its girdle of water, was hard, naked, rusty moor, with a group of men digging black peats out of it not a bow-shot from the greenest of its embowered meadows!

Aagaard is the work of a fair number of centuries—eight or nine, maybe; yet after Aagaard there is hope even for the Alhede district and the Great Vild Mose, with their hundreds of square miles of barrenness in the heart of Jutland. And the Danes perceive this, and, encouraged by the prodigious recent growth of their trade with us in agricultural produce, are talking about reclaiming these immemorial wastes, as well as draining their inland seas. While our home farmers have despair at their elbows, the Jutlanders are merry with hope. "Long may our appetite for butter and bacon continue!" they exclaim, " and may the prices descend no lower than at present."

They have tried sending milk into London from Esbjerg, and mean to try again and again, until yet another industry has been opened to them. Hitherto their success in this line has not been encouraging. On the average the voyage to Harwich takes thirty hours. Add two or three more hours for the journey to London, and as many for the collection of the cans within but a narrow radius of Denmark's port, and it will be seen how badly the word " fresh " will apply to the Jutland milk thus thrown upon the thirsty metropolitan market. Freezing, however, will make a difference, when our Danish cousins have perfected their dairies so that cleanliness is more in the ascendant with them than it is even now. As for cream, where is it so rich as it is in this green land of our marauding forefathers? Once let Danish cream get a grip of our affections, and Devonshire herself will take a second place in order of merit.

But it is time to ride on. Aagaard, with its cows and its romantic surroundings of viking tombs, and the red-saddled church of Kjettrup across the shallow valley, is a tempting spot to tarry in; but we must away, with that warning note of our landlady's still resonant in us.

A mile further, and the populous village of

Fjerridslev is entered, with a bright little district hospital by the roadside, and a baker, a blacksmith, a carpenter, and the other simple tradesmen of a community to keep it quite independent of the influence of the big towns. Fjerridslev is on the main great western road between Thisted, the capital of the *amt* of that name, and the much larger town of Aalborg. It is about five-and-twenty miles from each town, and Lögstör is its nearest point to the railway. Hence it has to stand on its own legs as best it can.

There is a thorough-going old-fashioned inn here, with a lengthy red front and rings in the walls for carts and horses. The Fjerridslev girls in the summer go about with footless stockings; one of them took me to the inn, chattering prettily the while, with her eyes riveted upon my radiant "Sunbeam." Though so remote from urban civilization, these villagers have not the air of rustic blockheads. There is such bustle here, and as large a variety of passers-by in wagons, carriers' carts, and chaises, as in the old coach days rejoiced the eyes and understanding of many an English Boniface, whose hostelry now stands high and dry out of the broad current of life. While I dined at Fjerridslev, one vehicle after another pulled up at the door, and the uncorking of bottles and the clatter of mugs and glasses was incessant.

In the large coffee-room a trio of mellowed old gentlemen opened a sort of bank for an hour. They all smoked large china-bowled pipes, drank beer, and laughed very much, while they shuffled bank-notes. The round-armed maids who bustled about in the room jested with them freely, and they in turn jested with the visitors who came in and added to their stock of money. I hope they were itinerary bankers, but it is just probable they were only officials collecting the king's taxes.

The wind was now as lively as it seems mostly in the mood to be in West Jutland. When I rode forward, it gave me all the assistance it could until I came in a mile or so to a forbidding by-way with the name "Kollerup" on a board. This was the beginning of woe. For the next six hours, my "Sunbeam" was in the main a sad encumbrance.

Kollerup was quite near, in an upland basin, with wild-looking moor all round it, and an interesting church. An indeterminate mechanic was in the churchyard, with a chisel in one hand and a spade in the other. He let me into the building, and, still with his hat on, he whistled cheerfully as he drew my attention to its antiquities. Of these the pulpit was the chief, a wooden hexagonal construction of the year 1599, with odd carvings in white wood on a ground of dark wood, illustrative of Christ's history. White and gold columns divided the panels, and a huge sounding-board overhead suggested to the pastor, perchance, that he was bound to make his sermons as excellent as in his power lay. But in a tray by the pulpit steps were several buttons and metal discs, collected from the alms-box, which bore witness to the spiritual imperfection of the parish, in spite of the spacious sounding-board. My guide paused in his whistling to laugh as he fingered one of the buttons and compared it with those on his own waistcoat. But he seemed very shocked when, on the strength of the resemblance, I ventured to upbraid him for having yielded to the temptation of humour and irreverence in conjunction. He assured me he had never done such a deed as that.

A very ancient granite font, circular, on a low plinth, and two family pews with the date 1590, made up the other more obvious charms of Kollerup's church, which has besides a fine glowing exterior (whitewash), and a high vaulting, groined and domed. Some pleasant houses nestled about the graveyard, but beyond all was wild and bare.

Then for three miles I climbed by a mean sandy and stony path from upland to upland, in a tearing wind, with nothing in sight but the tombs of incinerated vikings and their lieutenants. I was making straight for the North Sea shore, but no sign of it or aught else save larks and ravens appeared. Three garrulous maids with school-books passed me on their way south, with the wind rosy in their cheeks and playing tricks with their short frocks. They smiled, dropped curtseys as pretty as their cheeks, and we parted.

High up on the moors, with the sand now almost as white as salt, I looked down at length upon the church of Hjortels, and a scattered hamlet of white houses. Beyond was the Jammerbugt, or Bay of Lamentations, with a snowy landward fringe to it far north and west. Even through the clamour of the wind I could hear the riot of the waves breaking upon this deadly strand.

The church of Hjortels gave me a lee wall to breathe by for a few minutes. I have seldom had such a bustling as in this climb and descent to its white body.

Then came another mile of ups and downs by a mere bridle-path, and I was on the edge of a steep declivity of sand, with a foreground beneath of white and olive-green hummocks, over which, before the shrieking wind, there hung a thin veil of what seemed to be vapour, but was only the loose sand of Lamentation Bay, flying from mound to mound before the breeze.

It was all collar work here. My "Sunbeam" sank in the soft stuff, and but for the lure of a bathe in the glorious breakers of the North Sea, I should have hesitated before facing such an amount of it.

Endurance, however, was never better justified. I passed a lifeboat station and a cottage or two set between the sand-heaps, with an impertinent black dog on guard; also some stalwart boats; then one solitary bathing machine; and afterwards I had all to myself one of the most amazing great bays in Europe, glowing white both ways, as far as the eye could carry, and with an indigo sea thrashed into foam thundering its waves in endless lines upon the sand.

Denmark calls it a bay, but that seems taking a liberty with a geographical expression, for there is no converging headland to the north, while west the chalk cliff of Bulbjerg completes only the faintest effort of the land at a curve. The Jammerbugt is, in fact, no bay, only a white open strand some forty or fifty miles long; and mightily the North Sea waves must enjoy the sport it affords them, whether they have a disabled ship in their clutches to toss on the sands at leisure, or whether their pastime, as on this day, is as innocent as that of porpoises at play.

A vigorous hour in the water and on the hot sands, and "Sunbeam" and I were ready to retrace our tedious steps. From what I had read about this Bay of Wailing, I expected to see barnacled wrecks decorating its sands to the horizon each way, and at least one poor drowned body just washed up. But there was not a tincture of the harrowing in the picture it made for me. All was boisterous, bright, and sunny. If a corpse had come bounding forward on the crest of a wave, I should have expected to see it break into laughter as uproarious as that of the wind and the water.

It were better now to have returned direct to Aggersund after this introduction to the white cliffs of Svinklöv. Instead of that I made for the east from Hjortels by a winding road, always with its attendant burial mounds near or less near. A poor road at the best, and seldom fit for my " Sunbeam." It was up and down, with little to see except the brown pimpled moor and a rare farmstead with a girdle of low shrubs deformed by the wind.

When the afternoon was waning fast, I called at one of these farmhouses and begged for a glass of milk. But the farm lady declined to give me so common a beverage: I counted eighteen fine cows and a bull in the neighbourhood. She honoured me with home-brewed beer, and watched me drink it. Viler stuff never asked the palate to cry "Excellent!" but it was liquid and I was parched dry. Had it been kerosene, I believe I should have smacked my lips over it and looked just as gratefully at the generous lady. In these moorland houses the dogs are not polite beasts, and all the time I drank, my hostess had much ado to keep her yellow hound from flying at my calves. A mile past the house I could still hear the disappointed rascal giving tongue about me.

By Lerup the country of a sudden blossomed into a green vale, but this depression was not for me. I had come through one Svenstrup, and now I entered another, more thirsty than ever, and sighing for soda-water even as my "Sunbeam" craved a good road. But more home-made beer was my portion instead. A good-natured small farmer with whom I exchanged some words no sooner heard to what nationality I belonged than he armed me into his house and called his wife. A quart bottle of a liquid made of elder flower was put before me, and I was urged to drink it all. It had not a particle of sugar in it, yet I obeyed their kindly invitation. And I answered as well as I could all the questions they put to me into the bargain. For patriotism's sake I was sorry to have to say "No" to my entertainer's assertion, for the good of his wife, that London was as large as Denmark. But I was rewarded for my honesty in the loud approval of the lady. She turned on her spouse, and almost called him "fool" for ever harbouring so absurd a notion.

Here, at Svenstrup the second, I struck a tolerable road. But alas! the wind was furiously in opposition, and I was eight miles yet from the Aggersund inn and the roasted pigeon. I am loath to say more about my weariness (from pushing and battling against the wind for hours) than this: I could have dropped asleep by the roadside at five seconds' notice.

I worsened matters by a mile or two through taking a wrong turning. The road was hardly ever level, mostly uphill—or, I fancied it,—and there were times when I thought I should have the added worry of a thunderstorm full in my face.

Torslev, Lövsted, Haverslev, and Beistrup were passed with great toil and greater thankfulness. They made little mark on my mind. Beistrup pleased me most, as being the nearest to Aggersund ; by no means for its church, whose graces seemed statingly modern.

Once I sat on a stone heap to enjoy the spectacle of Aggersund itself. It was all I could do to get myself off those stones : the bliss of inactivity seemed the best gift in Heaven's cornucopia. And in the end it was a very jaded adventurer who staggered into the presence of the girl with the freckles, the dimpled cheek, and the blue eyes at the Aggersund inn.

It went to my heart to grieve these good people in the matter of the roast pigeon. But I was not fit for such a banquet. While my landlady lamented for all hearers about the cursed invention of cycles, I gave myself wholly to soda-water and apologies, and then I climbed the ladder staircase to bed.

CHAPTER VII

Travelling merchants—A delightful road and midsummer
weather — Aabybro *kro* and village — The Great Wild
Moor—A comfortable inn of the old style—Sunset over
the meadows—Evening pastimes of Aabybro.

IN the remoter parts of Jutland, such as Aggersund
and other places hereafter to be visited, the Englishman on tour need think little about his pocket.
There are no mendicants; prices are all low; and
robbery, whether in the highways or at the hands of
designing landlords, is not likely to put the glamour
of romance upon his travels.

I had already become habituated to the expendi-
ture of an occasional penny in a glass of brandy or
other spirit; and now, from my Aggersund bill, I
learnt that a man need pay but two shillings for a
sufficiently good bed and his breakfast of eggs,
bread, butter, and coffee, including several serene
glances of a pretty maid while she did him service.

None the worse for my fatigue of the previous day,
I was on the road at nine o'clock the following
morning. The sun burned above me, and I had no

anxiety about the weather. To-day, at all events, I did not mean to adventure on paths marked in the map by mere thin lines instead of the double score of a long-established thoroughfare.

Once more I entered Fjerridslev. Its inn was as clamorous as before. A spectacled *handelsmand*, with a wagon-load of sample cases, was preparing for a campaign among the farmsteads and stores of the neighbourhood. He had an immense variety of goods, from Namur cutlery to Nuremberg cuckoo clocks. Nothing at all English, I am sorry to say. His merchandise was spread about one of the long tables of the inn, and gave the place the look of an immature bazaar. The gentleman drank Pilsener and smoked a large cigar while he sorted his articles. He paid no heed to the eager-eyed maidservants who buzzed about him like gnats, with an evident lust for scissors and Geneva watches, with two yards of German silver chain to each watch.

Then, again, I went forward on the high-road to Aalborg, smiled on by such weather as makes the cyclist glad. Ever the larks overhead, no mud, no ruts, but little dust, a wind astern, the sun as bright as June and the farmers expect it to be, and the perfume of clover and cut grass moving with me for miles! With such a battalion of blessings, I could forgive the country its lack of sensational elements of the picturesque.

Viking mounds there were, of course, near and in the distance, so long as I was in the uplands. But after Svenstrup I was among pastures nearly as level as a sheet of paper, with no hills beyond either. A church here and a church there; for the rest, square miles of grass and rye and poppied barley; red-roofed farms and occasional villages, each like its neighbour; and to each village one tall factory chimney, token of the local dairy, in which day and night work goes on churning cream into butter for England. The jingle of the milk-cans was the noisiest feature of my run. The cans were either being collected by ones and twos from the outlying farms for the dairy, or they were being taken back to be duly filled afresh. A more methodical industry there could not be, and in all the lush clover-sweet meadows the Jutland kine stood about in pretty groups, or lay chewing the cud as if they knew their importance.

Bratskov, Öxeby, and Langeslund were thus approached, entered, and passed through, the country folk saluting with most cheerful air. The farther I ran the flatter the land became, so that there seemed no end to the horizon north and west. South and east was the silvery gleam of water; the Nibe Broad in the great dividing water-way. I tried to make out the islands of Öland and Gjölland, but they were so near to the right that there was no spying the thin channel of mud and water that but just detaches them from the solid mainland. Gjölland, however, was conjecturable from its fine square-headed camp. The ancient Cimbrians on their perch here had a masterly outlook for miles, and only the shrewdest of night marches could escape their vigilance. But of the two islands, Öland seemed the more attractive in the dense forest which covers the greater part of it.

Langeslund has a church the Calvinists of Wales would approve of. They might have built it, so different is it from the characteristic local edifice of whitewashed granite with a tower and a red saddle to the tower. There is also a *kro* here, devoted to the non-alcoholic faith. They sell sweet ale and milk, and inside is a sort of warning to those who love spirituous liquors and common bottled beer. But the place was delightfully clean, and the parlour they showed me into would not have made a princess uneasy about her environment.

If anything the road improved as I went on. No fault could have been found with it, and my "Sunbeam" exulted in its agility. Thus it was quite early when I came to the river Rye and the famous Aaby bridge, with its equally famous *kro*. The bridge is of wood, and the river flows muddy and deep under it towards the Nibe Broad, some four miles distant; and the *kro* stands a hundred or two paces from the bridge, near the Aaby dairy, with its tall chimney and jingling machinery. There is a goodly homestead facing the *kro*, a blacksmith's shed handy, and a store where they sell you a basin or a pound of tea. This is the village of Aabybro —"bro" meaning "bridge." Aaby, with its church, lies two-thirds of a mile farther east. The vast green, hedgeless country surrounds the Aaby *kro*.

I was to see much of this pleasant inn. For the moment, however, I was only concerned to order dinner in an hour or so. The landlord looked as if he had been born an honest innkeeper : ruddy of face, handsome, and with great shoulders. His wife was about twice his own breadth, and, like himself, was ruddy and strong. They had a small daughter, round-eyed and merry, quite a ball of a girl, though full grown. This was just such a trick as Fortune loves to play us mortals, who confidently expect what we seem to have a right to expect. Such a husband and such a wife ought to have had a giantess for a daughter. Happily the virtues and comeliness are quite independent of adipose.

A short hour sufficed to take me to Aaby village and back. The road was better even than before. The bridge is a junction for Thisted, Aalborg, and Lökken, and the ten miles between it and Aalborg are of an excellence in keeping with their importance. I hoped my "Sunbeam" would prove their merit,

but it was not to be. The church of Aaby stands
on a mound, with good trees near. A base desire
for my dinner sent me hurrying back when I had
cursorily viewed its white exterior, and the flower-
beds among its graves.

The Aaby inn parlour was almost a state apartment. Beyond, however, was even more magnificence; a blue drawing-room with gilded lamp, knickknacks, photographic albums, and German prints on
such sympathetic texts as " The first kiss," and " The
last sigh." I forgot my cycle and fancied myself at
Rosenborg. And the little Metha waited on me,
bringing me lamb cutlets and new potatoes, and
afterwards (for the first time in Denmark) that truly
national delicacy, strawberries and cream. The
potatoes and strawberries were the earliest gathered
from the inn garden. My heart went out to my
landlord for this tribute of beneficence.

Then I smoked while the girl prattled, slowly, so
that I might the better understand her. She showed
me the family albums, and herself from the beginning
of her photographic career as something very small
in a woman's arms; a brother, too, who was in
America, but had not answered anticipations; her
bosom friend, a refined, engaging girl of her own age,
who lived only across the road, and whose father had
made much money in America. And then she was
called away by the bass voice of her mother. It was

Metha's lot to serve the populace with its corn-brandy and coffee and beer in the spacious common-room of the inn. She was only the barmaid, though her father's daughter, and he patently a man of means. To rise at five and work all day until ten at night, and then, after a romp with the maids on the dewy grass in the garden at the back of the inn, to go to bed at eleven ; such was her daily routine. Yet no carolling canary in its cage was more cheerful than this little Metha Jensen of the Aaby *kro*.

Though brute inclination urged me forcibly to enjoy luxurious idleness under the old walnut tree in the winsome garden of the inn, with perhaps a game of skittles in the alley adjacent, I could not on so glorious an afternoon remain rooted in this vivacious spot. Back again my " Sunbeam " and I sped to Aaby village, and then by a long coarse road we ascended a very gradual slope of land with houses where it culminated. Thus, in much less than an hour, I came to Bjersted, and leaving it behind reached a lone burial-ground, with a church just below, while yet farther below was the vast bleached surface of the Great Vild Mose (Wild Moor), an area of bog and turf level as a billiard-table, some fifty miles square, without house, tree, or enclosed space upon it. To me, lying on a viking mound conveniently near, it looked like a dried inland sea bed, crusted with saline deposit. Hopeless for agriculture as it is now, it will be taken in hand sooner or later and turned into splendid grazing land. East and north white farmsteads by scores press upon its edges, as if the canny husbandmen were forming about it to be in readiness for its acres when these have been made cultivable.

Only the turf-cutter now-a-days ventures upon this barren waste. The black dots of his peats showed thickly on the south fringe of the moor, like inky hailstones dropped from the clouds; and he himself was visible toiling on the torrid shadeless tract. Anciently it seems that this Great Vild Mose was quite other than it is now. Where the foot cannot tread without peril of being ingulphed in the quagmire, tree-trunks are standing erect, though submerged. The whole district has in fact subsided and been planed smooth by water action. It remains for our generation or its successor to drain and dam it and revive its old fertility. But modern Jutland will then devote it to cows and barley, not to the oak woods which clothed it when subterranean disturbance began the epoch of its ruin.

The Great Bog of Jutland proved not at all the ugly, depressing spectacle I had thought to find it. Those sentinel white buildings on its margin were its redemption. Besides, on a day like this, there was something exhilarating in its length and breadth. A man does not get dwarfed in his self-esteem by a life on the prairies. There is the more room for his individuality to expand over. This whitened waste had a kindred effect on me while I lay stretched on the heather of my perch, with two chattering magpies (I am glad they were twain) flitting between the church wall and the church tower, and bees voluble in the warm air about me. Of course, too, the Jutland larks sang their eternal melodies high towards the blue zenith; and, late in the year though it was, I could hear a cuckoo.

The temptation to descend to the moor was somewhat severe, yet resistible. I did not relish the return journey with my cycle on so hot a day. Doubtless, too, the Vild Mose, like many a Spanish city on its hill, would not improve on a closer acquaintance. It were an idle aspiration, but I should like to have known if, when they buried the Dane over whose bones I rested, the landscape from his tomb was much as I saw it, saving the presence of the farmsteads. It probably was, if forests be substituted for the pastures and grain that now bound the moor. The Great Vild Mose, like Babylon, became contemptible many more than a thousand years ago.

I took myself back to Aaby, much to the joy of the magpies, who made blatant protests about me so long as I continued on the tomb.

Here things were at the high-water mark of

activity. A cluster of vehicles stood at the inn door. One was a ridiculous old family carriage, with crimson velvet cushions and two long-tailed steeds in the shafts. The lady and gentleman who had driven up in it were in my room taking tea, and the coachman was indicating to a carrier the compensating features of his unwieldy wain. Two carriers' carts stood at ease behind the family chaise, each with a packed human cargo, whence the blue smoke from several long pipes rose in a mist which hung lightly above them. Now and then the little Metha or an assistant bare-armed maid ran from the inn with bottled beer or *aqua fortis* for the travellers. There was also a diligence killing time, as diligences will in the north of Europe as well as in the south. A huge wagon, piled high with boxes, trussed goods and barrels, came behind the diligence. It suggested the migration of a village, but was really only a delivery van from Aalborg railway station ten miles away.

But the most assertive of these wheeled obstructions at the Aaby *kro* was an open dray full of pigs. As pigs they were faultless—clean and fat, and with intelligent countenances. They seemed, however, thanks to their intelligence, to have painful premonition of their fate. Having been born and bred in Jutland, they resented this forced journey to a slaughter-house, whence they were to travel to England in quarters. Their cries were indeed so acute

that I fled to the skittle alley for relief, thus ex-
changing a throng like Cheapside's for such sweet
tranquillity as you may find in the Temple Gardens
at six o'clock of a summer's morning.

Nailed to the trunk of the walnut tree was a
board on which "the honoured public" were begged
not to walk on the grass borders. I was spelling
forth this request when my brawny landlord came in
haste to me from his coffee-room, which judiciously
looked back and front. On no account was I to be
deterred from walking on the grass if so I pleased,
he said. "One has all sorts at an inn, you understand—and it is for the other ones." The good-
natured man was not content with this effort to put
me right at my ease.

"Come," he whispered gleefully, and his eyes
took an arch light that became him curiously.

He guided me from his pleasure-grounds, with
their rose trees, stocks, pansies, arbours, and skittles,
into the adjacent more practical pot-herb garden.
Here was a small strawberry bed. Down he bent
among the leaves, then stood up triumphantly and
offered me a ripe berry.

"You shall find others," he whispered; then
laughed, nodded, and ran back to his customers. I
had not been treated thus paternally for many a long
day. The honest fellow! his hospitality was better
on the palate than all his strawberries.

And from behind a scullery wall or something of
the kind the roseate countenance of his blooming
wife smiled approval of her goodman's act. When
I looked up from my second berry, there she was,
wagging her head at me with most positive en-
couragement.

While I supped there was a continuance of the
earlier bustle outside the inn, with the added
element of cows. The first batch of pigs had gone
on to the butcher, but there were others. And the
way these later arrivals wailed in concert with the
lowing of the kine !

"Do you not get weary of such a noise?" I asked
my little handmaid, when she removed the *débris*
of cold slices and brought coffee and cognac.

But to Metha it was a case of the merrier the
more noise. Her day's work was nearly over. She
had already put a ring on one of her fingers in preparation for a brief junketing ere she was off to bed.
One thing more she told me.

"The Sunday that comes is St. Hans' *fest*, and
we are all going to dance in the evening. It will be
splendid."

At ten o'clock I went forth to the bridge over the
river Rye. The air was now crisp in spite of the
flames in the western sky, and the water smoked.
Over the great meadows, too, a thick white mist was
rising, and catching the crimson of the sky. Through

the vapour, towards the manor-house north of the road, I could see cows by fifties capering before the cowherds, who were urging them into their stalls for the night, and their bellowings were tumultuous. This manor-house, like that of Aagaard, has gone in roundly for cow-keeping. Its precincts, closely wooded, and girt by a dyke and some semblance of a moat, made a forested island in the midst of the flat treeless and hedgeless meadows.

Somewhat later the inn maids also came to the bridge, arm in arm. They were such magnificent personages in their low-cut gowns and assuming strut, that I did not recognize them at first. Like myself, they were drawn to the water by a mere sentimental attraction; at least so I fancied. But even while we commented together on the sky and the cows, I espied two manly forms breaking through the mist Lökken way. Then off, with a short curtsey, went the girls towards their lovers; no longer strutting now, but anxious to use every moment of the time left them ere their strong-minded mistress sent them to their beds.

I gave the bridge entirely into their hands and made for my chamber. The inn was now shut, but from its garden sounded the liveliest laughter and cries. Metha, her enormous mamma, a strange young lady, and two other damsels of the house whom I had seen dressmaking in a large room, were all frolicking on the dewy grass. It was excellent to see my landlady's unwieldy shape dodging the others round the trunk of the chestnut tree, while she held her skirts high above her stout ankles. As my windows looked directly upon them, there was no escaping this display of ankles.

A syphon of soda-water and a bottle of brandy had been placed by my bedside instead of a candle. Really, were it not for my bright, patient companion down-stairs, resting its tyres in preparation for its toils of the morrow, I should have felt inclined to assuage with the cognac the momentary fit of loneliness that seized me in the sight of these innocent revels, in which I had no part.

But when eleven o'clock sounded in the house the mirth all ceased, and one by one the inmates of the Aaby *kro* came up to bed. This night I heard the gentle breathing of a girl on the other side of the partition to my room. She might have been one of the maids or she might not.

CHAPTER VIII

A temptation overcome—Jutland at its best for the cyclist—
A disturbing sight at Saltum—Lökken and its sands—
Hjörring — An obliging cyclist — Unwelcome ups and
downs—A fine finish to a successful day.

"To-morrow," said Metha to me at breakfast, "is
St. Hans' day. Will you not wait for it?"

The morning was superb. Her father had been
out in his meadows to cut grass at five o'clock, just to
give him an appetite for the more ordinary duties of
a landlord, and he pronounced the weather settled. I
was sure my "Sunbeam" would not sanction a delay
in Aaby under such conditions, even though it might
benefit by the rest. Still, I was tempted to temporize.

"Where will you dance?" I asked.

"In the wood on the island," she replied.

"Wood! Island! I do not understand."

"That is our way," said Miss Metha, as if it were
an idiosyncracy of the Jutlanders, of which I ought
to be envious rather than critical.

"But is it not difficult, among the trees, and, I
suppose, on grass, at least?"

"It is not on grass at all, but on white boards put up for the purpose, and there are lamps hung to the trees, and father's own cart will take us all, with a very large number of bottles of beer."

"Oh! And will there be many young men, Metha?"

The girl smiled.

"More than I shall want," said she.

I decided not to stay for the dance in the wood, which, on consideration, seemed to me a very heathenish custom. In all likelihood Metha's fore-fathers and foremothers, in the days when King Alfred ruled as well as he could in England, made love to each other after a ball among the oak trees. A sacrifice or two in honour of Odin and Freya would precede the revels then; and perhaps a troll would require to be conciliated with some dire ceremony.

Still, the picture was a pleasing one, and made Jutland and the Jutlanders seem a trifle less phlegmatic and matter-of-fact than they had hitherto shown themselves. The "bottled beer" was the least acceptable feature of the business. An orgy of Pilsener or Carlsberg at midnight under the stars and Chinese lanterns did not strike one as quite the ideal way to spend a Sunday evening, even though St. Hans was responsible for it, and the beer was from Herr Jensen's own cellar.

It was not easy to settle my account at the Aaby inn. Metha referred me to her mother when I asked for the bill, and Fru Jensen said her husband had gone to the village. I could pay the next time I was passing, both ladies consoled me by adding, as an inspired after-thought.

"But supposing I never again come to Aaby?" I inquired.

To this question Fru Jensen shook her shoulders. It was a problem she was too fat to attempt to solve.

Their united indecision cost me an hour of the morning. Then, however, the excellent landlord came in with a streaming face, mentioned four crowns (4s. 6d.) as an amount I might give him or not, as I pleased; after which, with handshakes and good wishes, we parted.

Jetsmark was my first village north-west from Aaby. I had seen the Jetsmark carrier's cart already—a lumbering object, stuffed with stolid women hugging baskets, and which required about fifty minutes for the stroll between the two villages. The distance is four miles, with a road admirable in every way. Larks, the scent of hay, a blue sky, a murmurous breeze from the south, cows, fields of barley and rye, scarlet with poppies and azure with cornflowers, and cheerful peasants with rakes and other implements of agriculture, some also with portable beer-barrels: these were the attendant and

I

comforting spirits of my thirteen-mile run to Lökken
on the North Sea, by way of Jetsmark. I crossed
the river Rye, which shone like copper, and other
lesser streams, its tributaries, and sped through the
hamlets of Pandrup and Ostrup; nor paused until I
was at Saltum, about half-way to Lökken.

Here an alluring highway travels east to the main
great north road between Aalborg and Hjörring, the
capital of the Hjörring Amt, to which this extremity
of Jutland belongs. But it was not for me. I had
first to pay my respects to Saltum's red-crested
church and then continue in the direction I had
already come.

This church proved of considerable interest. Its
charms at the outset were, however, of the ghoulish
order. While my "Sunbeam" leaned against a
rectangular family tomb in the graveyard, I groped
by a broken wooden door into a subterranean chamber
of the tower. Accident led me there, with some
degree of inquisitiveness also. Only a weak chink
of daylight stole into this apartment, where I
found myself stumbling so that a match was required.
Then, I confess, not without shame, I realized what
I had done. The clatter of wood that had followed
upon my forced entry into the place meant the
shifting of a coffin-lid. My match twinkled on the
mummied body of a child which lay in its last cradle
by my knee, with folded hands and its small legs

crossed at the ankle. It lay in much inodorous dust, and its eye sockets were full of the same simple and wholly inoffensive substance. I covered the little object afresh and looked round about it, only to see just such an ugly litter of the cribbed and cabined dead as I had seen at Björnsholm. They lay one on another, or on end, lolling against each other, upside down, or anyhow; and the floor was bespread with the fragments of wooden angels and decorative work which had once given the things something of an artistic look. Inscriptions on silver plates and copper plates were to be read, in spite of the tarnish of a couple of centuries: polysyllabic flatteries and such titles as come to the "high-born" without effort or merit. Still, there was little to keep me tarrying in such a hole by match-light, and I left it somewhat peremptorily; to startle, quite without intention, a couple of decent old peasants, man and wife, who had, I imagine, come into Saltum for a day's pleasuring, and whose slow footsteps had led them to the church. The woman was the first to perceive me, breaking forth from the death-chamber. She lifted a gloved hand to her heart, exclaimed, and with her other hand pulled at her spouse. But I made haste to inform them that I was as much alive as they themselves, and that it was only an indiscretion that had taken me among the dead. They received my words with a mystified air, but were fain to be convinced of their import as

I gave my attention to the other details of the building.

Saltum church is domed and white within, the chancel domes being piquantly painted with arabesques of a wild kind. There are flowers and flourishes, and, bowered amid their curves, fruits, devils, Cupids, cherubs, archers, beasts and birds with human heads, and much else, may be seen perched with the profusion of a Christmas tree. It is fancy let loose, much out of keeping with the staid whitewash of the place, as well as, I wot not, with the sober-faced Jutlanders and their black-garbed women-folk who come hither on Sundays.

But there was something more here. The two peasants were ejaculating about them, with uplifted fingers and enlarged eyes. By the north wall of the church, on several roomy shelves, were arranged a startling collection of relics of church decorative images of pre-Reformation times. Headless, legless, or armless saints; saints with broken noses; saints with sword-cuts on the folds of their wooden garments; also a very large wooden Crucifixion model, with the Virgin and St. Joseph flanking it, the colours still fairly preserved, but the group itself hideous in its ruin. Whoever is responsible for this exhibition may be set down as an injudicious person. These halves and quarters of effigies, which had no merit when in their prime, affect the imagination hideously. They make the church look like an ill-furnished museum of anatomical monsters, and do credit to no age; neither the one to which they belonged nor this latest age, which, like the good peasants on holiday bent, stares at them with painful wonder.

The Saltum pews and the pulpit are the best things in the church. They are tastefully carved in the Palladian style, and date from about the middle of the seventeenth century.

In the remaining seven miles to Lökken, I passed through but one village and troubled no church. The country became gradually less green and the grain less robust. I was again in the sphere of the North Sea's influence. Towards the left sandbanks showed, with olive-coloured grass on them, and long before we rode into their midst the red roofs of the aspiring little town were visible in their setting between yellow sand and blue sky. The thunder of the North Sea's waves was far louder than the comparative mildness of the weather seemed to require.

Lökken's streets are all sand and pebbles—and cod's bones. The place is engaging in its disorder. Its streets do not pivot neatly on trim squares, but start as a rule where they please and end where they please, and the houses have the same unconcerned, independent air. I saw here the meanest huts I had yet seen in Jutland, with dissipated-looking women brawling in their precincts, and close by was a spick-and-span hotel or bath-house, all gorgeous in red brick, white stone, and silken and damask upholstery. It was not yet open, but the shadow of its accomplished magnificence had well preceded the arrival of its swallow-tailed waiters, its German manager, its French cook, and its English tariff.

The town, which is really only a fishing village, though anciently the third port in Denmark, huddles close under the sand-heaps cast up by the sea. Some of the houses will assuredly one of these bad nights be overwhelmed by the sand. But dwellers by the ocean generally view with great composure the mere possibility of such perils as this.

At the inn here I was met plump with as good English as one may find on a cosmopolitan mariner's tongue, the mariner not being an Englishman. The landlord, a gaunt fine fellow, with just the limbs for lifeboat work, had been fisherman ere innkeeper. He had lived for eight entire months at Greenwich, for some unapparent reason; and this experience in particular had put him at discord with his Jutland home. Nevertheless, back to sandy Lökken he had come, to his wife and daughter; and in sandy Lökken he was now quite prepared to spend the remainder of his days.

" We are all fishing men in Lökken," said he, " and we most of us have some English."

The man told me that his little town meant to make a bid for European esteem in the holiday season. There was to be a railway from Hjörring, some eleven miles inland. The Bath Hotel was already fit and well; the Lökken streets were to be re-arranged and kept as free as possible from sand and fish-bones; and of course some bathing-machines should be made.

"There is not a more grand seashore in the world for people that like the water," he added forcibly, turning afterwards to a black-haired man with rings in his ears, and begging confirmation of his words, which was promptly given.

I had not seen the coast yet. The loose sand-bank against the houses looked so formidable a barrier. But now I went out, with permission, to spend a quarter of an hour on the shore ere dinner would be served.

And he was right. Lökken is a continuation of the wonderful strand of the Bay of Lamentations. The scene was the same here as there, *plus* the convenience of domestic accommodation close at hand. The same matchless rollers racing upon an infinite length of the finest sand in the world. "Infinite" is of course not exactly the term; but forty or fifty miles are to the common biped quite a sufficiently large cut out of the illimitable.

It was as invigorating as it could be. And the

best of it was, that no sooner had I clambered to the other side of the sandbank, than Lökken was as good as expunged. One lone bathing-machine was here as at Svinklöv, and also there were some boats drawn up. Else, I might have revelled again in the glorious solitude of that lower part of the "lamentable" yet very fascinating bay.

What would not such a shore-line be worth in England, anywhere within two hundred miles of the metropolis? We have, however, nothing to compare with it, scarcely even a sample of such immensity.

At Lökken they gave me very greasy soup but aldermanic turbot. My landlord talked with me while I ate, and his daughter cooked and waited on me. She was a well-grown, capable girl; her father asked me if I did not think so, and I had no alternative but to trust my eyesight. He asked me also about a certain beer-shop in Greenwich, which I fear he used to frequent needlessly in the dead old days. Was it there still, and did —— continue to run it? But I am sorry that my education has not qualified me for examination in all branches of learning. I could not, if hanging depended on it, have told him the name of a single hotel or tavern in Greenwich, save that immortalized by the whitebait.

Then away my "Sunbeam" carried me along the best of roads (after Lökken's sand was done with) to

Hjörring, in the warmest hour of a cloudless mid-summer day. Everything was favourable, from wind to gradient, though this latter might be said scarcely to have existed. A casual hillock or two were discernible to the south of the road, one with the significant name of Baalhöi, or Hill of Baal. Near this height were also the conspicuous buildings of Börghun Kloster, which more than eight hundred years ago was a royal residence, and whence, like enough, ships were ordered to cross the sea from Lökken, to see what they could ravish from the English coasts. Rank cowardice kept me aloof from the monastery church: that and the blazing sun.

In less than an hour I was at the base of the hill of Hjörring, eleven and a half miles from Lökken. The red roofs of the town, with the greenery of its encircling gardens, looked very refreshing to a hot cyclist. Inside, however, Hjörring is nothing much, save a compact and cleanly provincial capital of seven or eight thousand inhabitants. Its streets were a trifle too steep for my " Sunbeam," and their cobbles were not to be endured.

Here chance took me for a moment or two (afternoon tea, to be precise, since there is no disguising the appetite begotten of a cycle) to the Hotel Scandinavien. The landlord's own machine was outside his door, and looked perfectly willing to be amiable, upon introduction, to my " Sunbeam," and the landlord himself was eager to be my mentor in all local matters, when he learnt that the stranger who had ordered tea was both Englishman and cyclist. He told me, with pride, of the five score and more "wheelmen" in his town, and of the club of lady cyclists, restrained by no petty provincial prejudices from wearing knickerbockers when the fancy seized them. And how greatly his life was inflenced by his machine, he informed me in telling of his holiday experiences from London to Edinburgh only the last summer, and of his designed tour from Hjörring to Flushing a few months after my visit.

But there, I need not dwell on this familiar tale of Denmark's affection for the cycle. From the highest of her people down to the poorest, whose means will yet indulge them so far, they are mostly bitten by the fashion, always assuming that they are not residents in the wild west whence I had come, and where the average cyclist of, say Hjörring, Copenhagen, or Aarhus, would as soon think of riding as I of attempting the Grampians on my "Sunbeam."

I had still eleven miles to go before I could consider myself anchored for the night. An ordinary pedestrian landlord would have tried to dissuade me from a farther journey that day; he would have ensnared me into sleeping in one of his own beds. But this gentleman was a sportsman and conscientious. Still he need not have made so very light of that final eleven miles in the fag end of an evening.

Nor did I appreciate very highly his resolute declaration that he would accompany me part of the way. He said point-blank that he had had no exercise that day, and that it would therefore give him the greatest joy, etc. At my best I am no scorcher, and I did not relish the prospect of straining to keep up with this accomplished long-distance tourist, to whom a run of a hundred miles between breakfast and evening dinner was no more than a whet to the muscles. But there was no help for it, and I could only beg him to be merciful, and to remember that whereas he had kept fresh and cool during the hot hours in his spacious shaded café, I had borne the blaze of the day. In my heart I hoped he would be beguiled from his kindly purpose by an attractive pair of knickerbockers in the town streets, or at least a divided skirt.

My knowledge of the Danish character was, however, incomplete, since I could suppose this gentleman capable of putting me at a disadvantage. True, he leaped and bounded ahead of me over the unpleasant paving-stones of the town, and for the first time in Jutland I felt constrained to try this urban pitching and tossing. Yet afterwards he was sweetly soli-citous of me, and bridled his energies in a way that won my regard. He climbed with me to several sharp road-summits, and left me at the last and highest of them, whence I had a view north of such hillocky country as I had thought to see no more of until I got south of the Lim Fiord.

It was as beautiful an evening as the heart of man could desire, with a soft golden light over the rounded hills beneath and on either side of me. These were not great hills, of course; but I liked not at all the thought of climbing them one after the other, even with the enlivening sequel of as many brisk descents as toilsome ascents. They were cumbersome enough, moreover, to hide the distant landscape, at the furthest point of which was my night's lodging, Tversted on the seashore. Nor were they, apart from their eccentric irregularities, at all engrossingly picturesque. It was the old scenery— treeless moor, only broken and billowy instead of divinely flat. I would rather have had them flat and ugly for the remainder of the day; so, in my weakness, I assured myself.

But at Bjergby, which means the town on the hill, though it is only a village, the trouble came wholly to an end, and I was thenceforward in full enjoyment of the silvery lining to my overpast cloud. The village stands nobly on a green cliff, with an old church in its midst. There were some rude chisel- lings in the red granite to its porches; notably a

loose-limbed dragon with a strange mirthful eye;
and the contrast of its dark ruddy walls and the
very white mortar that held the blocks together,
was as strong almost as that of the black and
white masonry of Florence. Its situation, however, with the broad mellowed champaign at its
feet to the north, was its best and most satisfying
feature.

Hence to Tversted—some six or seven miles—I
careered from terrace to terrace, until I was on
sea level, with a friendly neighbourhood of green
meadows, cows, and swarthy country-folk. Plenty
of bog land too, with black peat water in the
ditches, and cotton-grass sending its snowy tufts to
seek their fortune before each little puff of wind.
Farmsteads innumerable besides, and one cosy manor-
house, that of Odden, in a thicket of trees.

The day had, after all, kept its serenest and most
sportive minutes for the last. In my comfortable
vacuity of mind, and with bodily fatigue all gone
(ousted by the near hope of supper), I whistled in
accompaniment with the larks, who made their
usual mad music over me.

So by Uggerby church, and a little afterwards by
Tversted church also, where a dame with a black
kerchief about her head was putting the finishing
touches to her broom work for the morrow's service.
Then, with a rush, into a little hollow, where a bridge

spanned a stream in which two distressed geese, tied leg to leg, were striving in contrary directions, and up and round a corner into another hollow. Here some eight or ten houses nestled, one with the invigorating word *kro* over its modest portal.

CHAPTER IX

Tversted on the sands—A drab for a hostess—A worthy ex-
    seaman—A sad night—Unpromising weather—A novel
    ride—Wrecks—Rain—Old Skagen.

TVERSTED is nearly the end of the world—one of
its numerous ends, or beginnings, if you prefer it.
Nevertheless, five or six hale Tversted folk were
giving tongue in clamorous joy over a rusted and
misused cycle of an antique type, from which the
youngest of them had just fallen headlong. A singularly unkempt and unwashed-looking woman, with
blousy hair about her brows, was clapping her hands
at the inn door, in evident delight at the catastrophe.

The apparition of my high-born "Sunbeam" into
such a circle was much as if the horse Isinglass
were of a sudden to be cast into the company of a
couple of Whitechapel screws. A solemn silence
seized the Tversted men, and the ancient cycle stood
trembling—whether with jealousy or excusable
respect I know not. Every human eye in the scene
centred upon my pretty "Sunbeam," which I gave
freely to the fond caresses of their admiration.

127

It was not a very nice *kro* at first sight. But I liked it less even than at first when the blousy lady at its door, having answered somewhat too enthusiastically that I *could* have a bed in it, turned on me with a gleaming eye and inquired:

" Sure now, you'll be an English gentleman yourself ? "

I replied in the affirmative, with more cordiality than I felt.

Then ensued a series of mental and spiritual capers on the part of the landlady of the Tversted *kro*, for such she was.

Not for many a month had she had such a turn, she declared. An Englishman, and in her house !

" John ! " she screamed, the others watching her with open mouths.

" What, another Englishman here ? " said I.

" You shall see, sir; begorra, you shall see him."

It was now my turn to stand a-tiptoe with expectation. I wanted supper, but was content to be satiated beforehand with surprises, if these were of the desirable kind. Who could John be ?

But down tumbled the fond edifice of impetuous fancy when a short, stoutish man shambled outside, with a nose so brilliantly carmine that he could have lit his way with it in the dark better than with any cycle lamp I know. His eye came round the corners shiftily. It was absurdly as if he feared to see two officers in blue, with their truncheons handy.

This was John, and, as Heaven willed it, my landlord. My disappointment and hunger were at such a pitch that, without great work, I could have exhaled a tear.

They were British born, both of them. The man had spent ten years in a gasworks, and the woman, having been born in Limerick or thereabouts, entered domestic service in Cardiff, where she met her blooming fate in John at the gasworks. John, I understood from his other name, was an Englishman. Therefore, the strangely shy girl who was their offspring, and who was now hurriedly told to get some supper, was almost a representative member of the great British nation.

John had acquired his red nose at the gasworks, and he found inn-keeping at Tversted, on the tip of Jutland, the very best possible of callings to keep it in countenance.

I could be excessively eloquent about the dirt and squalor and general lopsidedness of this Tversted inn under British management. But why foul a nest in the reputation of which my own national pride is interested?

The place was not wanting in good cheer. They served me beef broth, seasoned as they season soups in Denmark, but do not in England, and with stewed prunes in it, which made me sad; also a roasted pigeon and new potatoes; later, more prunes. Indeed, I fared very well if I could but have been forgetful of the omnipresent dust and its entomological consequences, and of my countrywoman's appallingly grimy and dishevelled aspect as she handed me the courses with an unending stream of chatter. For years and years they had been at Tversted (how they got there remained a mystery unillumined), and I was the first of my race whom they had been called upon to entertain. God was, it seemed plain, very good to them at last.

All which, I feared, meant a bill as stately as the pleasure of which I was thus the blind, predestined instrument.

Meanwhile, my "Sunbeam" had been locked up with ceremony in a very large chamber, with seats and flags decorating it—the kind of room devoted in England to sixpenny teas for excursion parties. The Union Jack occupied a conspicuous place in the room, much to my landlord's credit.

"They shall not touch it," said my landlady, alluding to the Tversted denizens and my "Sunbeam."

After supper I felt grateful, and prepared to escape from the environing dirt into the evening air, now crimsoning under the sunset. But it was not yet to be. A bearded, handsome man was thrust upon me (against his own will and pleading, as was abundantly evident), with the injunction, "Show the English gentleman that you've not forgot the English you learnt when you was at sea." There was nothing for it but to encourage the poor fellow. I did this with a sigh, a bottle of ale, and a cigar; the sigh not for him, but for the sunset.

Yet really, in the end, he was genuinely welcome. He was a well-informed ex-mariner, now a freeholder, with cows and ryefields like his peers; and with every minute the English tongue became more glib to him. He told me of his various adventures of a more exciting kind, when his life was spent on the salt sea, and in so appositely circumstantial a manner! For example—"When I was on the Norwegian brig *Björnsen*, in the year 1884, one March morning, the ninth it was, and the time five o'clock, we being then mighty close to the Bill of Portland, with a strong south wind blowing, and a fool of a man at the 'hellum,' etc., etc." To tell the truth, he rather overweighted his narratives with their prefaces, though these gave them a most convincing sound of veracity.

Furthermore, he too, like all other retired seamen, was not so contented in his new condition of life as a mariner ought to be who has done with the perils of the crafty ocean. He complained of the price to which butter had dropped.

"There'll not be a living in cows soon," he

lamented; and said, astonishing me, that he and others of his class preferred the manufactured margarine of Odense to the butter from their own beasts, not wholly from motives of economy either.

"But anyhow," said I, "you have precious few taxes in Denmark."

"Too many for all that," quoth he, springing at this new grievance like a cat at a sparrow; and straightway he waxed voluble about the iniquity of divers abandoned old men of his district who, at the age of sixty, availed themselves of their statutory privilege, and, having assigned all their savings and other property to their eager children, cast themselves upon the parish, and successfully pled poverty. Very naturally too, he cried aloud about the hardship, that in A.D. 1895 there should be such things as estates exempt from taxation. True, I imagine there are not many such lingering relics of the mouldered old times; yet those that exist are large, and are in the hands of great men who could well afford to pay their dues. But of course Denmark is not wholly a constitutional country; and even under a benevolent despotism there must be a few trials.

My guest, in fact, thoroughly entertained me, while the villagers outside continued their painful pastime on the antiquarian bicycle, which threw them heels over head with excellent impartiality.

But at length he rose, and excused himself from trespassing further on my time. The phrase was most inappropriate, and so I told him. Then we clasped hands, and he recurred to his more congenial comrades in a row on the bench outside the inn, in whose presence the youngsters were hazarding their tender necks. John the ex-gas-operative was in the middle of the bench, with a pipe and (as I would have wagered) some bottles, full and empty.

There was still time to get a short glimpse of Tversted's surroundings ere the coral hues faded from the sky. How well the soft crimson light suited the desolation of the sandhills, which kept the North Sea within bounds here as at Lökken and Svinklöv! A red lifeboat-house warmed itself in the gentle radiance; so did the red tenements of Tversted.

I was too late to get to the coast, which is a good mile away, over abominable sand. There was, indeed, little left to me except commonplace slumber, after one more cigar with the villagers.

But the slumber I obtained was not commonplace. It was dream-haunted, as it deserved to be under the inspiration of my surroundings. For all the room I could have was a loathsome attic, with no window except a hand's-breadth of glass in the roof, a nasty ceiling, and such bedclothes as made me shudder when I saw them by a stronger light than that of the very small candle my landlady, with immense discretion, gave me when I retired. The mattress was as uneven as the country between Hjörring and Bjergby, and my head lay at an angle which kept it between twenty and thirty degrees below the level of my feet.

In the morning I execrated the Tversted inn, and descended the stairs to shake its fleas and other insects from my body. John was not out of his bed, but my landlady was ready for me, with coffee and kindly hopes about the sleep I had enjoyed. It were useless to distress the poor unkempt soul with reproaches, and so I paid my bill without a word, and steered my "Sunbeam" into the open as if things had been quite as they ought to have been.

It was a different morning to those with which I had of late been favoured. No blue in the sky, a disturbing stillness, and the look of settled or worsening gloom in the south-west, where the North Sea lay, and whence the wind was to make itself felt.

Sunday, too! And my plan for the morning to ride along the sea sands, to reach Skagen if possible in time for the opening of its church doors.

The day was warm and thunderous. Until I had pushed my way through the sandy ruts between the heathery heaps for the mile that separated the inn from the sea, there was none of that freshness of air

one demands from a maritime village. But the
sandy defile came to an end, and by a declivity
softer than all before it, I reached my smooth high-
road. The waves were dark, and broke upon the
sands with a very decided sullenness. The ships in
the offing redeemed the scene somewhat from its
gloom; yet for all that I liked not the portents.

I had a good eighteen miles of running to cover
before I could hope to come to Old Skagen, which
guards the west side of the Skaw, even as New
Skagen, facing the Cattegat, guards it on the east.
There was scarcely the least likelihood that I should
see man, woman, or child by the way, for there is
no village between Tversted and Skagen, saving
Kandestederne, which, like Tversted, lies a mile from
the coast, the sandhills of which isolate it with
great success. Moreover, I was not at all sure if
my designed route was feasible all through. There
might be a cliff intervening, which could be passed
only at very low tide; or the sand might turn to
shingle, and make fools of us both.

This I did know, however, that the sand of the
long nose of Jutland called the Skaw, is in parts
"quick," and warranted tenacious and hungry enough
to absorb a moderate horse and cart. The knowledge was useful, perhaps; but with so sombre a
sky, and so unfriendly a sea, it had the effect of
chilling enthusiasm to a considerable extent.

The more I stayed pondering, the less I cared for the programme I had planned. And so I cut hesitation off at the roots by mounting where the sand was firm, and making a trial trip. It behoved me to run as close as possible to the wash of the receding waves, that I might get good hold, taking my chance of the spray and the skittishness of the one or two unmethodical waves which every minute or so sped farther inland than their predecessors.

For half-an-hour it was pleasant, very pleasant. In the main, I could have wished for no better track than this shore, unmarked by the least track. Where modest streams entered the sea through miniature cañons in the sandhills, I had to go right through them, whether my tyres liked it or not. I was soon thus wetted well above the knees; and there were indubitably spots where, had I gone slow, I might have sunk a foot in three seconds. But these were, after all, trifling hindrances, and at every turn of the wheel I was getting nearer to Skagen, and seeing more plainly the schooners and steamships approaching the deadly neb of the Skaw, or diverging, having passed it from the east.

Certain things about the course I did not care for. Of these the chief were the suggestive skeletons of the ships that had come ashore here, and been done to death by the North Sea waves. They were right in my way, or high and dry, or as much as fifty paces out in the water, their black ribs still seeming to make a desperate fight with the sea that growled about them. I should think I passed a good score of these mournful objects. Here was the true Bay of Lamentations, this final curve of Jutland's lone peninsula. The vessels that drove rudderless on this desolate coast in the fury of a westerly gale could have no lamp of hope to cheer them, and the cries of the doomed sailors would reach no ears on shore. Certainly, topping the sandhills, I did see one huge iron brazier, and another at Tversted, which in wild weather serve feebly as beacons for the five or six and twenty miles of coast between Lillehede and the Skaw. But there can be little help in such puny bonfires. The ship in the clutches of the storm would learn from them the name of its executioner, not much else. Only afterwards, the casual fisher-folk would slip from the interior by their sandy defiles, to number the corpses, and see what material and permissible profit they could draw from the storm.

No, I liked not these dead ships, deep set in the devouring sand; with gulls, looking like battle-field birds of prey, perched on their salted timbers.

There were also innumerable small relics of ruin about the sand—morsels cast up by the sea, as if it had found them too tough or too childish for its seasoned old maw. In one hollow of the sand an infant's "go-cart" of tin, with the horse still in the shafts, a top near it, as if there had been two little babes at play when the crowning wave took the vessel in hand. Life-belts now and again; an enormous quantity of rape-seed, littering the sand for miles; not a few champagne corks, which made one think of man's fine recklessness in drinking when Master Death had already touched him on the arm, and pointed towards his grave; and, most moving article of all, a half-knitted stocking, with a bone needle still fast in the wool.

It was not very gay work guessing at the stitches in the history of these various bits of jetsam, nor very sensible pastime either. But I found my mind bent that way, and preferred to let it please itself. And besides, it kept me from fits of personal pessimism, which would else assuredly have annoyed me, when, about ten miles from Tversted, and as many from Skagen, the rain began to descend with great earnestness, and there was not a ray of promise of better things in the black heavens.

The Skaw meant "Sunbeam" and me to remember it.

Where Kandestederne keeps a few boats and a shed, I sheltered briefly to see if the weather's mood of ill-humour was transient only. But it gave no hint of such civility. There was nothing for it except to glide on, and be thankful that I had not

to put up with a cross wind as well as a pack of
ill-conditioned clouds.

There ought to have been a growing charm in
the growing nearness of the many ships of the
nations now passing by, almost within hail. But
that charm was lost. The lesser craft tossed much
in the broken water. I envied not the voyagers,
whether they were on the wet decks, or lurched to
and fro under the decks. And that was the sole
element of solace their spectacle afforded me.

Right glad was I when, drenched to the skin, I
came to the lowly cottages of Old Skagen, snuggled
among the sand-heaps, with wires strung between
posts in the enclosed spaces before and behind the
cottages, and ill-smelling fish pendent from the
wires. It was a grey scene of discomfort out over
the water; nor was the inland prospect much more
bracing.

Sopped as I was, there was no lingering to be
done in Old Skagen, which has been shorn of its
earlier importance by the uprising of the other
Skagen. But the most tedious part of the morning
had yet to be endured. I had to trundle my "Sunbeam" in the constant rain across the two miles
of sand and scrub which separate the two Skagens.

At noon, or thereabouts, the long line of red
houses of Denmark's most northern town was close
at hand, and I was thankful.

CHAPTER X

At the Skaw—A notable hotel—Tourists—Jutland's end : a
memorable scene—Open-air dancing—Rain and wind—
The sand-choked church—Bonfires, and strawberries and
cream.

ABOUT Denmark's most northerly settlement in
Europe (putting Iceland and the Faroes out of
count), Mr. Murray in his guide-book has made a
slight yet pardonable error. " To the long straggling
town of Skagen," he says with some impressiveness,
"the railway will never penetrate." These words
were printed ten years ago, however, and King
Christian's nation has since then had an unwonted
impulse of energy; the result whereof is seen in
the apparition daily from the sand of the south of a
large toy engine, with some toy compartments tailing
after it, all which labour into the heart of Skagen,
where there is a very neat railway station, and there
rest for a considerable time until the way-bill sends
them off again.

Thus had my portmanteau travelled to the Skaw,
or I hoped so. The article had not an enviable

journey from Esbjerg. Still its entrance into Skagen
could hardly have been more woful than that of its
lord.

The rain pelted in shafts upon the long but fairly
firm street when I pushed my "Sunbeam" between
the symmetrical and quite comely cottages of the
town. Not a human nose was outside save mine
own. But many human noses were at the windows,
and I was disagreeably conscious of my half-drowned
plight.

Of course Herr Bröndum's hotel was so situated
that I had to show myself to the best part of Skagen
ere I came to it. One expects these little taunts of
fortune at such times. I passed one hotel with a
warm, dry look to it, but it was not Bröndum's,
though the landlord, of whom I inquired, gazed at
me as if he were in the mood to equivocate. His
bottles of crimson and yellow cordials in the bar,
all but, of their own accord, lured me across the
threshold.

Then, somewhat later, I espied a high red building
with an English air, a little removed from the main
street, and set towards the Cattegat. This was my
bourne. Some groups of ladies and gentlemen, with
macintoshes and umbrellas, and the unmistakable
tourist demeanour, were about its precincts, seemingly cursing the unkind sky. If I did no more for
their souls, I put them off the scent of such purpose-

less misconduct, for I was in a worse pickle than they. But their pity or scorn (though this latter sentiment is more foreign to Scandinavian nature than to British bosoms) was wasted on me. I had now the wherewithal for exultation. Herr Bröndum received and welcomed me, and I was soon puddling my way up a clean, broad pine-wood staircase and into a bedchamber of metropolitan luxury. Hither too came my portmanteau, and the white-capped maid ended her angelic visitation with warm water. From my windows I looked on a number of glistening red roofs, much sand, a lighthouse, and a strip of sea in as pretty a state of leaden perturbation as ever evoked anxiety in the heart of a fisherman's wife, whose bread-winner chanced to be a few miles off the land. There was a dreary moan of wind too, with the requiem note strong in it.

Well, this was downright characteristic Skagen weather, at any rate. Thrice had I passed that sandy headland to the north ere thus setting foot on it, and each time it was to a fusillade of squalls, with rain and much tossing. And the white-capped maid had made light of my footmarks on the cleanly stairs, with words implying that such troubles were quite customary up here.

I ate an early dinner down-stairs to compensate for the inadequate breakfast of Tversted. There was no lack of creature comforts, and the dining-room was about the most seemly in Denmark. Artists from many parts of Europe come hither to paint ships and the moods of old ocean where she breaks upon the land. They also find the Skagen fisher-folk picturesque; what with their ringed ears, thick jerseys, peaked or skin caps, jack-boots, and well-kept little red cottages, with patient ever-young cabbages in the sandy enclosures fondly called gardens, their drying fish, and the sandhills tumbled about at the bidding of the winds. Herr Bröndum's hotel has profited by these invasions of the men of the brush and pencil. The dining-room is, in fact, a bright picture-gallery, its walls panelled into spaces, which have been deftly coloured by many hands in many different ways. Here a girl's head; next the damsel a seascape, all green and white and blue; then a fleet of Cattegat fishing-boats sailing before a gentle wind; cloud studies, face studies, and much else, with an historical group or two and some portraits of a more individual kind. No conspicuously bad work has been admitted to these walls; and most of the pictures are such as to enliven and aid digestion during a meal, and give the start to conversation afterwards in those blank moments that first ensue between attention to the needs of the body and those of the mind. The occasional gory morsels in the collection are not so obtrusive but that they can be disregarded without a strain on the eyes.

Under these civilized influences I soon forgot my late distress. There were guests in the room while I dined: Swedes from Göteborg smoking and drinking, and a portly lady in red velvet, whose walk was a revelation of majestic possibilities, and who might have been a real queen or a stage princess, but was probably only a burgher's wife. And outside the window chestnut-coloured boys in blue jackets were braving the rain with little boxes of shells and star-fish, which the visitor, taken greatly unawares, and perhaps with a very soft heart, might be persuaded into purchasing. One such was secured under my observation. He was stout, elderly, and wore a white hat. He seemed hard to please, and eventually carried off an entire collection of marine odds and ends. When he was gone, the little lads sniggered freely. But I was glad to see the coast triumph over the self-sufficient town here at Skagen, precisely as in a hundred mentionable places at home.

From the-dining-room two other rooms opened: the one a small *salon* for the ladies, with a piano and red tapestried chairs; the other for us coarser beings, with newspapers and ash-trays, telling of our coarser appetites.

But, rain or no rain, I declined to hive myself in these apartments.

Herr Bröndum had a little English.

"It is a misfortune, this rain," he said, "because to-day is St. Hans' Day."

"And do they dance here too?" I asked, mindful of the little Metha footing it in the wood.

"Yes, they will dance—that is, the common ones—by the wood. But it is for the evening that it does injury. We have fires on St. Hans' Eve. It is a great *fest* in Denmark."

"Then if it stops all will be well?"

"You shall then see much to pleasure you in Skagen—I hope," said Herr Bröndum.

The names of certain English artists who appreciate Skagen were told to me, honoured names. In the opinion of one of them, there is no place to compare with it for pictorial value, not even the Thames mouth and stream between the Nore and the Tower Bridge. For cycling, however, my landlord had no good word to say about the Skaw. Perhaps there is not a more unsuitable district for wheels in Europe. The sand does its best to cover up the railway, and it would not require a very amazing storm to wipe out the town, even as, just six score years ago, the old church was overwhelmed, so that now only its tower stands above the yellow heaps.

I clambered by the sandhills between the houses to the Cattegat shore, convinced that the now-vigorous wind would soon quench the rain. The sight was very inspiriting. The eastern sky was densely blue-

L

black, and from the horizon great waves came
tumbling one over the other, as if mad to get across
the Skaw headland and attack the North Sea beyond.
But they broke futilely on the sands.

A number of bronzed fisher-folk were about with
pipes, eyeing the water. The lusty squalls shook
the very rings in their ears, but they themselves
were evidently used to such weather. They leaned
calmly against their short green palisades, and only
now and then tossed each other a monosyllabic
remark. Their offspring with shells and seaweed
were much more talkative, and it required some
very earnest Danish to persuade them that I could
not, on St. Hans' Day, burden myself with any of
their treasures.

For a laborious two miles I hugged this sandy
shore, which gave the very worst foothold imaginable. Periodically the gusts would seize on the
summits of the shore hills and whisk them away,
the next moment turning the eddies into my face
with a blinding slap. But the rain had stopped,
which was something. There were others also
adventuring like myself towards Jutland's romantic
end—ladies in black much incommoded by their
skirts, and several gentlemen with walking-sticks.
The ladies off and on vanished into one of the
dimples between the sandhills, to recover breath
and rest from the very real exertions of toiling over

such yielding ground. Nevertheless they got to the Skaw point ere I did. It was seeing them stand well off from the last heap, with the waves frantic on both sides of them, and their garments beating wildly about their persons, that told me man could no farther north in Denmark.

It is an impressive enough headland. Though flat as the horizon line, it makes its mark on the mind. For about two hundred yards from the last sand-heap a blade of yellow-white land runs towards the water, with the Cattegat waves fighting on one side and those of the North Sea on the other side. The sand slides into their midst and disappears. Over its submerged extremity there is eternal strife, as if for the possession of it. Even in calm weather this battle between the two seas is strong and unmis-takable. But on a day like this, it was within an ace of the sublime.

The waves tossed high against each other, endless battalions on both sides, reinforcing those that had gone down in the conflict. Their crashing made a din well audible above the thunder of the winds, and their shattered white heads flew indeterminately east and west, like a mad tangle of white hairs. A furious scene, and one from which the ships now visible, as if in an organized procession, kept well aloof. Behind this foreground of wrecked waves the funnels of steamers and the sheeted masts of tall ships moved slowly by, some to the east and some to the west.

The most capable of artists might set up his easel on this blade of sand, and never catch the atmosphere of the Skaw as one feels it standing here, tugged at by the storm winds between these two seas.

What a singular contrast, this Land's End of Denmark and ours in Cornwall! Yet, of the two, the Skaw is far the more fatal. You would suppose to be wrecked here were an experience rather akin to being thrown on a bed of down, so amply does the soft Skaw sand stretch itself for the reception of such unfortunates. But the great lighthouse half-a-mile away knows better than that. It is only when the waves have sucked the breath of their victims that they toss them on this easy couch.

I would not for much have missed the Skaw, now that I know what it is.

As for the lighthouse, it differs little from other lighthouses save in the mightiness of its organs of salvation. From its tower, nearly a hundred and fifty feet above the sand, you may see in a day more ships than the average lighthouse elsewhere sees in a week, and at such close quarters too, with the aid of the powerful glass they use. They need never be dull or monomaniac up here. Besides, the town of Skagen is accessible in twenty minutes by the more stable meadow of sand and scrub between the sandhills.

The lighthouseman who had me in charge knew something from experience of English lighthouses. He believed his home at the Skaw had nothing to learn from us. In the matter of wild weather too, he reckoned the Skaw could beat Cape Wrath or any of our stations. A moment on his balcony was enough for me this St. Hans' Day.

The town of Skagen is fully a mile long; but it is not as populous as you would suppose. Its houses are small and low, many only one storey high, and generous in the matter of gardens, as they may, for effect's sake, be called.

Towards the beginning of evening, I walked all through the town, debouching at the south into the country. Here was a mass of greenery which I had seen from the lighthouse and wondered at. And it was what it had seemed to be, the stereotyped parochial wood. One could only guess how they had got it started. But there it was, a nice thick collection of small trees, with summits planed absurdly smooth and even by the winds, and with narrow tortuous paths cut in it, yet so dark that it was as if twilight had come upon the land five or six hours before its time. Nor was this all. I had noticed many young persons of both sexes moving at a funereal pace towards a point at one end of the wood, and now the wind blew the faint squeak of a fiddle in my direction. Did Skagen also dance under the leaves on this midsummer eve?

It was not quite that, but the intention was plainly there. If the Skagen coppice had had an open clearing, no doubt the ball platform would have been set up therein. As it was, the merry-makers got as near the wood as they could. They had an enclosed space with garlanded masts round it, and three glum musicians stood under a bower of green stuff, which threatened momentarily to collapse on their harmonious heads. Perhaps fifty young men and maids were present. Most of them were inactive, content, it seemed, to watch the solemn frolickings of the others. But now and again the impulse to caper became more general, and then they made their platform throb. As they were all dressed for open-air exercise, and the young gentlemen danced without removing their pipes from their mouths, there was a certain artificiality about the proceedings. I really do not think they enjoyed themselves consummately, except when, between-whiles, they withdrew to an adjacent booth, with pink paper roses festooned above it, and ate gingerbread. The fiddlers were a very melancholy trio, but periodically these gentlemen came to a dead stop, and put a bottle to their mouths, first one and then another, nor resumed playing until urged by their patrons more peremptorily than politely.

From the glances some of the damsels cast at me, I almost believe they hoped I would join in their sport. But the thing was impossible. Besides, I wore such very large walking boots.

I wandered away from the dancers, skirting the wood, through small defiles of sand, the heaps on either hand thinly bearded with pale-green reedy grass. The clouds spat rain, but only intermittently, though with a look as if even now they could if they would do much worse.

It was painful plodding in the peppery stuff, and I was about to turn, satiated with such exercise, when I saw what I had hoped I might see. Stuck among this wilderness of yellow mounds was the *tilsandet kirke* of past Skagen : just the staircase-sided tower of the church for about half its height, with three small belfry windows to it, the lowest no more than breast-high above the sand. Its face seemed as clean as if it had been lately whitewashed, though thus interred to the neck, and its red saddle was still bright. But what a spectacle the thing was, thus lonely and abandoned ! A mere corpse of a church, condemned ever to keep its glowing white ghost above ground for the winds to howl round and the tired gulls to perch on ! Fifty feet under lay its choked aisle, pulpit, altar, the psalm-books and spittoons in use in A.D. 1775, and the graves of the old dead, with such an unexpected thick blanket betwixt them and the grey skies they had smiled upon in life. The Skagen sands have rare games with us mortals. They tickle, annoy, and infuriate us in the heyday of our vigour; open their long yellow arms to clasp us when the sea has buffeted the soul out of us; and in one mad mood cover up fathoms deep the holy house in which, among other petitions, we pray to be saved from the perils of the winds and the seas. There ought to be very special mention of them in the collects used by these north Jutlanders.

On my way back to the hotel, I searched the house-tops for storks. But none did I see. These diverting birds would, so far north, have to pay too high a price for their great wings. An unamiable hurricane might catch them thirty feet above the soil and hustle them off to England or Sweden before they had time to realize their circumstances. Besides, in the battle of life up here, the seagulls would perhaps join their unnumbered forces and terrorize any mere integer of a family of storks into a state of positive starvation.

An early dusk was upon Skagen when I reached the Cattegat shore of the town. The revels of St. Hans had begun here now as well as by the wood. Excited lads and lassies were rearing bonfires and lighting them in the teeth of the wind. Their parents watched them demurely, heedful more of past midsummer eves and fires long since burnt out. Four or five of the fires had got famously alight, and through the flames the children jumped and scurried one after another with shouts. One had evoked great admiration by running this gauntlet on his hands and knees. It looked foolish, but so did not he, with the glow of triumph on his face, until a tub-shaped dame slid from a sand-heap towards the fire and got him by the neck. This dame's arguments were of the shrill, quick kind. She aided them with slaps, but her drift was obvious. There was no particular heroism in crawling into the fire to burn clothes which the candidate for heroism would not have to pay for. After this no one else attempted to pass through the flames in question, save in the common way.

The jets of fire much improved the Cattegat sands. No matter if they were a little suggestive of wreckers' lights, and of ancient rites and ceremonies connected with the worship of the god Baal.

We were a party of twelve at supper in the hotel picture-gallery. The lady in red velvet was really a baroness, it seemed; but she much over-acted the part. We were all very decorous at the meal, though it was pretty plain that an under-current of expectation pervaded us. Two boys were of the party, well-mannered, as Danish boys of the middle station and upwards are wont to be. Yet it was all they could do to keep their furnace-flames from bursting out. Their eyes were like diamonds for brightness.

All which Herr Bröndum, who paid me the compliment of sitting next me, explained by telling how he himself had organized the best bonfire of all, and something besides; and that after supper we were to go in a troop, and, in the presence of the personages of the town, set fire to the pile, and subsequently enjoy ourselves.

This programme was achieved, though not without difficulty. The wind was at its tricks again, and it rained steadily. A German lady, with whom I chanced to be walking, had much to say about the delightful romance of the whole business. But there wasn't much romance or delight for Herr Bröndum and the other leading citizens during their long, vain attempts to get the tar-barrel in the midst of the wet shavings to marry itself to the torch. A crowd of about a thousand, or half Skagen's population, waited patiently for the ignition, which happened at last. Then loud was the roaring of the flames, and the Skagen youngsters screamed for joy.

When the fire was well in decadence, about a score of us recurred to a certain hut on the sands close to the bonfire. The Skagen children had for the past hour been sighing with desire on the threshold of this hut. Within was a table, a snow-white cloth, plates, silver, wine, biscuits, and strawberries, supported by a huge bowl of superior cream. Here we feasted, standing, as remote as we could get from the doorless portal. The strawberries and cream were of the best, and the sherry wine also was good. We drank to each other, and we drank to St. Hans. I have no idea, even now, who St. Hans was, but he must have been a very worthy gentleman.

It was about midnight, with sufficiently tempestuous weather, when we went to bed. The gentlemen did so mostly with cigars still between their teeth. The ladies looked as happy as innocent excitement may perhaps be warranted able to make them.

"Who was St. Hans?" I asked one lady.

But she was the German lady, and knew no more than I.

The night that followed was a wailing, shrieking, bellowing night, and its rain flogged my windows brutally. Without the steady red light of the light-house, the outlook would have been monstrously depressing. As it was, though I had given orders to be called for the first train of the morning, I had few and feeble hopes of being able to mount my "Sunbeam" on the morrow.

CHAPTER XI

The Skagen railway—The storm-tossed Cattegat—Aalbek—
Elling church—Frederikshavn—Running before the wind
—Saeby and its kloster—The hotel Dania—A scamper to
Aalborg, ending with disaster.

THE cyclist at Skagen may be considered a person
not bound by the common rules of social life. Like
the genius, according to modern interpretation of
him, he cannot help being a little or more than a
little insane. Hence, I do not think my brisk departure from the place the next morning was
imputed to me as an unpardonable offence against
the unwritten laws of decorum.

The fabulous dining-room smelt strongly of stale
cigar-smoke while I drank my coffee therein somewhere between five and six o'clock. That was the
trail of St. Hans.

"What weather to-day?" I asked of my waiting-
maid, who had assured me, for my comfort, that
she felt it no hardship to be up but three full hours
after the dawn.

"Storm weather," said she, with a nod of the head.

And yet, when "Sunbeam" and I moved away through the sand towards the railway station, it looked like nothing of the kind. The sea was quiet, and the sky was prettily enamelled in blue and pearl-grey. The air was good, very good. After its vigorous clearance of the day before, it seemed so pure that even the fish-heads on the coast, and the whole cods hanging so still from wires in the gardens, could not lift their wholesome perfume against it.

We crossed the little sandy square, with the monument in its midst telling of bravery and a wreck, and so came to the station, where the toy engine was playing at the game of shunt. Here my cycle was received with extreme respect, and given a nice slender iron pillar to lean against. Until it was lifted reverently into the compartment destined for it, the dear thing sunned itself in the admiring looks of several men and women of Skagen awaiting the train's final shunt into position.

The Skagen railway and rolling stock are amongst the most interesting objects in Denmark. There was a very big porter on the platform, who, I feel nearly sure, could have clasped the locomotive about its stomach, and moved it from one set of rails to the other. For us passengers it was much like getting into a rather large toy train, made to run twice round a nursery without stopping. The red-coated post-man and the consequential station-master, in the

fulfilment of their respective duties, gave the train a
certain fictitious dignity.   But one had one's doubts
about the afterwards.   Removed from the invigorating presence of their splendid uniforms, would the
little toy engine be able to keep up the illusion, and
actually carry us for miles, or would it blow up,
stop dead, or run amuck into the sand either to the
right or the left?

It behaved superbly instead.   To be sure, our
progress was slow, and distinctly drunken.   We were
nearly an hour running the ten miles to Aalbek,
and I was all but sea-sick when we got there.   Yet,
under the circumstances, the performance was
creditable.   You see there was much sand on the
line, and whenever we traversed a foot-road it
behoved us to creep, and if a man stood by the
notice-board that guarded the crossing, and solicited
a seat, it behoved us to pull up for him.

However, it was pleasant enough.   The carriage,
with its polished fitments and spittoon, was above
criticism, and the landscapes were absorbing.   The
tower of the choked church was the last thing in
Skagen I beheld.   But after that came sand-hills
and sand-ridges, peaked and rounded, sand in every
conceivable shape, daintily greened and yellowed
in places, and all domed by the pallid blue sky, with
the now-changing clouds of grey and slate mottling
the blue.

We ran into the district of the *dopper* and
rimmer, which also has much individuality. Here
the sand has been considerably raised by the wind
or man (or both together), so that it forms long
broad-based walls. Between the walls were strips of
the greenest and yellowest meadow-land I ever saw.
The yellow of the flowers in the grass was now and
again almost too bright for belief. It made the eyes
blink. But the effect was very pretty, especially
where a stunted farmhouse, with a red roof and a red
face, and a giddy little windmill mounted on its roof,
gave direct human interest to the scenes. In some
of the meadows, moreover, were ink-black cows—
another graceful touch.

This was more noticeable south of Hulsvig than
between that village and Skagen. And it was hereabouts that I began to shake my head, and to realize
that Herr Bröndum's maid might be only too astute
a weather prophetess. The Cattegat, which we
skirted, seemed smothered far out with dark shadows,
while inshore an ominous tinny glitter possessed it.
Long before Aalbek was reached, the white-caps had
risen on the water, and the wind was whistling
shrilly through the cars.

But there was this in my favour: the compass and
the run of the smoke from the farm chimneys showed
that it was a north-wester that was brewing. My
course could now only be south, with occasional

deviations south-east and south-west. I meant
therefore to spread sail merrily and enjoy while I
could.

At Aalbek they confirmed me in my beliefs. The
station-master scoffed at the train to which he was
a ministrant.

"You will be at Frederikshavn before it," he said;
"you can rest a little, and still beat it."

He had a cycle of his own, a poor old muddied
thing, which looked ashamed of itself by my
"Sunbeam," when he drew it creakingly forward.

"One must have what one can have," he
remarked with a shrug, after a minute's silent
comparison of the two steeds. His philosophy
heartened me as much as, I hope, it solaced him.

Level and wind suited my "Sunbeam" most
excellently. For three-quarters of an hour, we both
had a charming smooth run. The sand of the road
had sucked up all the rain, and was the better for
the draught: consolidated instead of loose. There
was more traffic about than I expected—drays and
cattle, and large women with their gowns held high
above their ankles: but nothing to hurt. And the
air was so sweet with clover; while, for companion
on the left, there was ever the moody Cattegat,
whose waves crashed upon the shore more loudly
every quarter of an hour.

The little villages we ran through on the flat were

remarkable for just nothing. Their names are Ledet, Jorup, Kragskov, and Niestrup, and when that is said all is said.

Elling, the last place before Frederikshavn, drew me aside to its church—white, with red saddle tower. My movements hereabouts intensely annoyed a very small dog. The little creature gave tongue and made for me, and, with a powerful show of diminutive white teeth, behaved like a viking of old. Even when I dismounted, and was looking through the church windows at the handsome full-rigged, three-masted schooner which, with sails all set, hangs in the chancel, the small dog had not done with me. He stood on a mound outside and bayed like a demon dog, with lusty tail action. An aged beldame from a thatched cottage near entreated the little object to be tranquil, purred to it and raged at it, all to no purpose, and when I was off again, I could hear it far behind me still exercising its tender lungs in long-drawn moans.

Of Frederikshavn I expected fine things in the way of shops and civic architecture. But it disappoints from that aspect. It looked as bright and well-washed as a good-humoured little child with an assiduous mother, and that was something. The man at the level crossing kept a young lady with school-books and my " Sunbeam " and me waiting an absurd time for a goods train that had been signalled to pass. The young lady protested she would be late, and I too deplored the idleness. But the official argued that he was responsible for our two lives (or three, with the " Sunbeam's "), and that therefore he would by no means let us through till the train had passed. He did so, nevertheless. Our united eloquence was too much for him when ten futile minutes had sped. The young lady, however, irritated him prodigiously by the suggestion that perhaps the train had gone the other way. Yet she may not have been far wrong. They are very droll about their railways in Denmark.

This town boasts some five thousand souls and the blessing of sea-communication with Göteborg. A winter or two back I was nearly crossing the Cattegat this way. I was already on the steamer in the Swedish harbour, waiting, with other passengers, for it to start. But the specified hour went by, and then another hour, and then part of a third hour. Only after so absurd a sojourn was intelligence brought us from the company's office that there was too much ice in Frederikshavn and that therefore the ship would not sail. This sort of thing may suit the temperament of Europeans of the extreme south and the far north. To me it seemed idiocy.

However, to-day " Sunbeam " and I did but look at Frederikshavn's port, which was beautifully trim, and with very few ships in it. The Cattegat now roared against the sea-walls that kept it aloof, and the offing was a frenzied mass of black and white water.

I drank soda-water and milk in a café, and learnt from the proprietor that the grave itself is hardly less tranquil than his native place.

"You should leave it and go to Copenhagen or America, if you do not like it," I suggested, casually enough.

"If only I could !" wailed the disconsolate man. " But I have many children."

Frederikshavn, though small, has, like the other towns of Jutland, disproportionately extensive suburbs. I pushed the cycle nearly a mile before I got to the end of the flag-stones, which indicated the end of the township.

Then up and away, with the gale behind.

From Frederikshavn to Saeby it is about eight miles, by a capital road which hugs the coast, and the wind saved me sixty per cent. of the exertion I was prepared for.

The scenery here was very bright. A green ridge runs parallel with the road landwards, and under it (sheltered from the impetuous west winds) nestled many a farmstead, their meadows and corn-fields extending east, with quiet little streams pervading them. These rivulets seemed not at all anxious to merge themselves in the turbulent

Cattegat. They moved at an extremely slow pace the nearer they got to the yellow sands.

So, however, did not my "Sunbeam" and I. Some of the squalls fairly swept us before them headlong, and smart steering was essential at times to prevent being volleyed at a cart, or a labouring man toiling in the opposite direction. I am generally well satisfied with a speed of ten miles an hour on a cycle, but this obliging north-wester would not be content with anything so mediocre. In about five-and-twenty minutes it shot me into the purlieus of Saeby; with such a zest too, that for many yards I ran on the paving-stones without finding it convenient to pull up.

The Saeby townsfolk were moving about with bowed heads and hands preoccupied with caps or gowns. I was pleasantly struck by the place, which looked yellow with age and withal clean and well-to-do. Also, it seemed abundantly supplied with hotels. One, Larsen's, was just such an old rambling hostelry as on a market day you would expect to meet fine old crusted countrymen in. I was, however, dissuaded from going thither to dine. The wood-turner of whom I inquired did not mind submitting a very bald head to the blasts that he might ensure my arrival at the hotel Dania.

The hotel Dania's landlord was an enormous lame man, who welcomed me as if I had been a good angel. At first he was not quite sure, but the word "Englishman" worked wonders. Then he clattered about with his walking-stick, and, having ensconced my cycle in a theatre that was attached to the hotel, with a robber's cave still mounted on the stage, he drove his cook before him into the billiard-room, where I waited. The lady was to categorize the contents of her larder, and I was to pronounce sentence.

What astonished this landlord was the fact that I could understand him and he could understand me. He exclaimed with rapture repeatedly. Nor that only. He cried aloud for his daughter, a small willing girl, and hurried her up the street. As the result, a sardonic-featured gentleman came to join us, and to answer the landlord's heated inquiry if it was not an indescribable marvel that I should know the Danish for beefsteak and strawberries.

"Perhaps the gentleman travels for butter?" demurred the visitor tentatively.

"Not at all," said I.

"Then he is certainly very clever," was the prompt response.

Pending the preparation of dinner, I was for seeing the once-famous church of the Mariested monastery, which now plays the broader part of parochial to Saeby. Nothing could be easier. The sardonic-featured man accompanied me as far as his office, whence the church — a red-brick Gothic building—was but a few yards' walk. It proved to be locked, and its churchyard a howling channel for the winds, which caught off my cap and gave me a run ere I could recover it. But there was an obliging grocer in a shop near who said he would go for the key. He wished strenuously also to go further to a certain humble coffee-house, where he said might be found an English sea-captain who, having brought coals hither from Newcastle, was now waiting for the Cattegat to settle itself suitably for his departure. I thanked the good grocer very much, but said I could see plenty of English sea-captains in England. He thought me an unpatriotic brute, out of question. That I minded not, under the circumstances. The little old woman in a black dress, whom the wind carried into the churchyard so very indecorously, was more to my taste, for she carried the key even as the wind had carried her. But she had to be allowed a pause of many seconds for the recovery of her ravished breath. Then only could she open the door.

The church of Saeby is a church indeed. Undefiled by whitewash, it bears with dignity and grace the decorations with which its Catholic founders endowed it. Its aisle is still lofty, and its one exquisitely groined and frescoed chapel might have but just had the word "*finis*" said of it by its

fifteenth-century beautifiers. There is no sparing of
colour here. The fine shafts of the pillars are
pencilled green and red; the window-lines are
colour-washed; there are many diverting picture
memorial tablets on the walls, the groups done on
the wood as fresh as if they were much less than two
or three hundred years old; and there is a fascinating old rigged and painted ship swaying gently in
the consecrated breezes which ever murmur between
these historic walls. The ship bears date 1645. It
may or may not be the original model of that time.
But·whatever it is, it is a most engrossing object
for the juvenile mind to gloat upon when the good
parson in his black gown and white ruff becomes
just a trifle dull in his sermons. The pulpit (date
1577) has attractive panels and sounding-board.
The pews are about a century later, and more
interesting than the average pew-survivals at home.
A carved altar and handsome candlestick also deserve
notice in this Saeby church.

To all these details my black-garbed guide would
willingly have drawn my attention had she not quite
early felt suspicion of my foreign birth. She spoke,
however, with such indistinctness that I had to
trouble her to say her little sayings twice apiece at
least. This was a great affliction for the poor little
lady. She clapped a hand to her breast and sighed;
mentioned bronchitis also, I believed. Of course I

offered her my sympathy, and among other things
told her of some simple palliatives for her complaint.
Whereupon, however, she opened her eyes at me
as if I had been an ogre. And from that time
forward she would not be persuaded to say an
informing word to me. Having murmured to herself, "Poor man, he does not understand me!" she
set herself rigidly to the task of not understanding
me. Her compassionate nods and sighs to my
crystal-clear inquiries made me laugh at length.
That finished my business with her. She went to
the door, and stayed there until I had done with the
church. Then she gave me plenty of elbow-room
for my departure, and took my thank-offering much
as a caged monkey takes a nut from a strange hand.

I was sorry for the little old lady and sorry for
myself. Afterwards I learned, however, that she
had quite lately lost her husband. If it was this
loss that she had tried so incoherently to tell me
about, small wonder the poor soul did not think
much of me when I recommended her to try certain
lotions and a mustard plaster for her ailment.

Before returning to the hotel Dania, I fought the
wind towards Saeby's little harbour. The town is
on as pretty a bay as any in Jutland, with a band-
stand mounted upon its low cliff walk, and at least
the shadow of a wood for the Saeby young men
and young women to lose themselves in. But on

this day the Cattegat was everything. The sea-captain from Newcastle showed great discretion in his preference of the Saeby coffee-house to this small sea in a temper. The long lines of rushing waves with broad white heads were far better to behold than be in the midst of. And the horizon was just about as black as cloud could make it.

I fared sumptuously at the hotel Dania. My landlord's ancestral silver had been cleaned in my honour. The butter-boat for the boiled turbot was of a size and pattern to excite desire, and the spoons were as captivating as Scandinavian silver spoons can be. The little daughter who waited on me was very nervous, poor child, yet happy in her responsibility. Even when she dropped the beefsteak, and brought upon herself a terrible succession of reproaches from her lame but copious parent, she seemed still as if she valued her office far more than she dreaded the risks it involved. As for the strawberries and cream, they were here, as all over Jutland in midsummer, a dream of epicurean deliciousness. When the meal ended with coffee and *aqua fortis* I felt profoundly reinforced. The bill was but two shillings, and I made the little girl quite radiant, I think, for four-and-twenty hours. The child, at her father's bidding, actually kissed my hand. Since she seemed as eager about it as her sire, I allowed her; for has not our great Ruskin written much about the ennobling effects of reverence upon the human soul? I am by no means really reverend, but perhaps none the less I served as an excellent fertilizer of virtue in the little maid's susceptible heart.

"Write in it that we have had an Englishman to dinner," said the Saeby innkeeper, when he stumped into my room with his visitors' book. This also I did, and I hope the information may profit both Saeby and the hotel Dania.

And now I was ready to start on an enterprise of the road that to Saeby, in the persons of my landlord and all with whom he spoke on the subject (and he button-holed thereon every creature that called in for a ten-öre beverage), seemed little short of raving madness. I had no protection against the rain, and the clouds were as thick and full of rain as a charged demi-john of wine. At any moment the bung might be removed, and then——

I set Aalborg before me as my stopping-place for the night. It was now past two o'clock, and the distance is twenty-nine miles, with no railway nearer than Frederikshavn, and only two wayside *kros* in all the nine-and-twenty miles. I was to gallop across the bleak yet not unfertile region of the Vendsysselers, a people in some respects comparable to the Somerset men of the seventeenth century, and who, like them, in past times have often fought

with scythes and pikes on behalf of what they conceived to be their rights.

"Well, sir," were my landlord's last words, "if you
will go, make haste, and come back some day."

I made quite remarkable haste. For the first ten
miles the wind was only half kind. Instead of
blowing full on my back, it caught me on the right
or north shoulder, often with such violence as to
spin me something like a teetotum from one side of
the road to the other, and to threaten me with the
black water in the ditch if I were already on the
road's left margin. But I soon learnt the trick of
tacking so as to get its aid, and there was no
question as to the respectability of the pace at which
I moved.

The hills were moderate until I was at Flauen-
skjold. The landscapes did not entrance. It was as
tame a district indeed as any I had seen—meadows
and fields of grain, with here and there a tree, here
and there a house, and but three churches to some
fifteen miles. Solitary, too. I disturbed a road-
mender, and passed two wagons full of ticketed pigs,
and that was about all in an hour.

Yet perhaps it was as well I had no temptation to
tarry. There was no mistaking the menace of all
the heavens to the north. At every lull in the gale
I felt for the first premonitory raindrop, and went
the faster to get out of its way. Before me was a

high hump of wooded land—the Jutland Mountain. This had to be crossed, and I relished not the possible programme of toiling up this slope with the storm, both wet and wild, taking me in the neck.

However, I got to Flauenskjold dry as when I started, and alighted for a little moment at the *kro* of the place. Here was a great tangle of resting drays, ploughs, mill-stones, and such other litter as you would only find outside a country inn ten miles from a railway station. Within, three gigantic Vendsyssel men in skin caps and heavy grey overcoats (strange gear for the end of June) were eating a dinner of surprising quality for such an inn. Another man talked with them, but did not eat. He threw dice on the stone top of a drinking-table instead. I also threw dice while I sipped my soda-and-brandy. But not for long. That Damoclean blackness in the north hung over my soul and urged me on.

If only I had had courage enough, I would have enlarged my designs of the day, and run from Flauen-skjold two miles east to Voergaard and its church, and back again to my main road. But I fought against this temptation to see one of Jutland's finest manor-houses, with its haunted chamber or cell, " the Rosodont," which has the knack of making its tenant confess his sins as easily as he might drink a glass of gin. The building is of red brick (Christian the

Fourth's epoch), with white stone facings. The glance at it I obtained, and the tower of its more distant church, contented me. After all, as I persuaded myself, I was in Jutland more for movement than sight-seeing.

And now I set myself for the mountain climb, which looked none too cheerful. But I had not taken into account the help I was to get from my friend, the north wind. While we crossed the lowlands at the foot of the ridge, this began to fume and bluster more vigorously than ever. The poppy in the fields and the rye-stalks were all bent one way, and stayed so, trembling under the strain. And it was thanks to the storm, which fairly lifted me at the elbows, that I went up the windward side of the Jydske Aas like a bird, without any sensible muscular strain. From the purple heather I passed upwards into a defile, between bright green Norwegian pines, and so out again on to the naked moor, and to the summit, whence I looked over a tolerably broad prospect of hills like billycock hats, not unprovided with my old and valued acquaintances, the viking pimples. But not one house was to be seen. Here, in the heart of the province, there was more pronounced loneliness than in the flattest and poorest of the western moors. Yet it was a scene to remember: the brooding blackness of the low-hung clouds upon the purple hillocks, a warm brown or yellow where they were not gay with flowering heather! The extensive woods of Dronninglund were discernible to the south-east, but not, I am sorry to say, the villagers of that famous manor. Between one and two centuries ago these rustics were wedded by their lord, the Brigadier Halling, strictly for purposes of racial improvement: to the strong man the beautiful wife, and to the mis-shapen man and imperfect maid, no wife at all and no husband.

Then for miles it was in the main downhill, among the heather and juniper of the moors. I went like a winged thing, and at little cost. Thus in an hour and a half after leaving Saeby, I set my brake hard, and stopped at the *kro* of Hjallerup, which makes a conspicuous red mark by the roadside.

"Sir," said to me here a country gentleman whom I had lately passed, and who paused at the inn to drink, "what is your opinion of our railways?"

I did not hint my true opinion, for I was not sure how sensitive a patriot he might be.

But he smiled for answer, as he put down the shawl with which he had covered his shoulders.

"Ah!" he exclaimed, "if God would give me my young years again! Then I would move like you. You were a spark, sir; I saw you, and you were gone."

· I told this to my "Sunbeam" afterwards, and the dear creature quivered to the compliment. The old gentleman and I drank a quiet glass of cognac together, and I bade him farewell. Only ten miles from Aalborg! It seemed a sure thing that I should yet escape the deluge that was just as surely advancing from the north.

Once more

> "The minutes wing'd their way wi' pleasure."

This for half-an-hour, until, in fact, having sighted the water-line of the river-like Lim Fiord, which was much outraged by the storm, I ran faster than ever towards Nörre Sundby, which is the suburb, on the north side of the channel, of Aalborg on the other side. I had felt for the first time that day a spot of rain. It was now to be a break-neck race betwixt my "Sunbeam" and the clouds. These last were a sight to see. To look at them was to be soaked, in fancy, from head to toe.

But at the one-mile stone (Danish mile) from Nörre Sundby, all in a moment down fell the fair castle of my hopes. I had ere this been conscious that my "Sunbeam" was slightly indisposed. Thrice had I had to pump air into his symmetrical body. Now, at the junction of the Saeby and the Hjörring roads, his hind tyre went flat, and nothing I did could swell it afresh. Meanwhile the enemy was upon me. Wind and rain attacked in concert.

For an hour and a half we walked, maimed and halt, in this humbling weather, past the pretty gardens and cottages on the outskirts of Nörre Sundby, and into that considerable suburb, with its many large old inns "for landsmen" and others who prefer here to stable their horses, rather than pay the dues over the bridge of boats into great Aalborg. It was a saddening, woful business, and so wet withal.

The fiord showed itself quite as agitated as it had seemed from above. Though but a third of a mile across, it was aboil with waves and spume, and the bridge set on the boats rocked up and down so that some wit was at times necessary to keep one's balance.

Thus we came into Aalborg, with its twenty thousand inhabitants, its spired cathedral, red-hulled steamers, and green-bottomed timber ships from Norway, its aged houses in narrow streets, and its metropolitan liveliness. Neither "Sunbeam" nor I quite liked civilization to be sprung on us in such a manner. We were a disreputable pair, fit only to crawl into a corner and there lie and mend or die, as chance pleased. But instead of accepting our proper doom, we made for the Phœnix, which every one assured me was *the* hotel for the stranger in Aalborg, and, having climbed a good elevation of very tiresome streets, came in sight of its swallow-tailed major-domo airing his stomach in the portico.

CHAPTER XII

I HAVE no very affectionate memories of Aalborg
on the Lim Fiord. That, however, is not so much
Aalborg's fault as smith Worsaae's.

And yet at first the town did not receive us any
too well. The swallow-tailed personage at the
Phœnix bowed very affably, and in the name of
his master deplored that we could not be accommo-
dated. While he spoke, sleek gentlemen of the
merchant persuasion went to and fro, in and out of
the hotel, all in a hurry, some with bags in their
hands, and some with letters for the post. It might
have been Lombard Street a quarter of an hour
before the closing of the mail. These accepted guests
looked down their noses at my " Sunbeam." It and
I were not at all in keeping with the fitness of
things at a high-class hotel consecrated to the
welfare of travelling merchants.

The Phœnix did not slight us really. It was

stuffed with guests; the major-domo took me to the chalk list of names in the passage to convince me. There was no giving the tablet the lie. To every bedroom the name of a Herr or a Fru was apportioned.

Then was I given in charge of a nice little boy in buttons, with a polished face, who had his directions to take me to the Nord, which is Aalborg's second hotel. The lad prattled prettily while we walked. As I was in no humour for conversation on general topics, and consequently not in the humour to understand his speech without more effort than I was disposed to make, to check him I put my "Sunbeam" into his hands to trundle. But he took to the task with the utmost volubility, nor ever ceased his innocent chatter until he had got me on the catalogue of the Nord.

Here all was well. The ostler was instructed, without a moment's delay, to push my wounded steed to smith Worsaae, whose reputation as a cycle-mender was said to be Jutland-wide; and then the head-waiter, in the most perfect English, talked me up to a spacious chamber, upholstered in crimson velvet, and entreated me to feel at home. It was an excellent room. I did feel at home. And supper was nearly ready. The only anxiety I had in the world was my "Sunbeam," and on that subject the head-waiter proffered me consolation.

" Yóu can, sir," he said, "rely on smith Worsaae
entirely. He is most respectable and very clever.
He is a maker of watches, but understands the cycles
of all countries."

On that I descended cheerfully to the dining-
room, and made the eighth at table to a very
satisfying meal, over which a landlord with an
obtrusive wart on his nose presided, with credit to
himself. The kitchen of this hotel made fools of the
cooks at all the other Jutland inns which I had
hitherto honoured with my presence.

Without feeling the least conceit in the avowal, I
may say that I excited much interest in this hotel,
which was not packed with merchants from porch to
attic. I was not a merchant myself (they soon got
that out of me), and I had travelled through Jutland
for pleasure. Jutland was not used to such flatter-
ing presences, and these her children appreciated
the compliment. But I did not play my cards as
guilefully as I might have done, when a white-
haired old gentleman, for instance, having evidently
nerved himself for the ordeal, chose a moment of
silence to spring on me an inquiry as to what I
thought most admirable in the country—"most
worthy of praise, you understand, my Herr." I
straightway flew at the Jutland winds and said
that they were unquestionably the most interesting features of the land. This was a mistake.

The face of the landlord (even his wart), the faces of the two waiters (including the one who talked English, and on the strength thereof seemed to feel a personal pride in me), and the faces of all the seven guests, were like the faces of men at a theatre, who, having looked up expectantly in anticipation of the lifting of the curtain, behold nothing but the curtain itself—as ugly a one, moreover, as any in the realm. And then what must I do, in my desire to set myself right with ten honest hearts, but flutter from the winds to the strawberries and cream ! The head-waiter at this had to retire : I was a disappointment. But the only reproof administered by the others was a gentle assurance from a round-faced man opposite, with his neck hid by his napkin, that there were just as good strawberries and cream in Zealand as in Jutland, and that he had also enjoyed the same dish in Regent Street, London.

After supper, the rain having ceased, and a bright, cool evening ensued, I strolled out to see the town, and smith Worsaae. The smith was then busy with a chronometer, and could only stake his integrity that I should have my " Sunbeam " as good as new early in the morning. I had full faith in his integrity, and dismissed him from my mind.

Aalborg has streets of mediæval houses, all or nearly all the ancient charms of which are lost to the

eye of the world under the coats of white and grey
wash, with which they are daubed, I should guess,
every other month. It is enough to induce weeping.
Such lusty old gables, and solid beam and brick
bodies to the houses, with curved gable-ends, and
droll gutter-spouts, and often inscriptions in archaic
Danish, with the date fifteen hundred and something
above the threshold, and pretty nigh the whole
smirched into a ghastly similitude of sameness by
the confounded whitewash! The streets ought to
be vistas of the past down which the artist or the
antiquary might gaze with glorious professional
thrills. As it is, if he wishes to know anything
explicit about these old houses, he must interview
the landlord and obtain permission to scrape away
the plaster of the last few decades.

It is heart-breaking, and the more so for the sight
of the two or three respectable antiques in the
Gammel Torv and the neighbourhood. These are
not defiled by the improver, and they tempt the
sentimental vagrant to stand and stare at them until
he has drawn others round about him, who cannot
help standing and staring in like manner. The old
mansion house of Jens Bang—delightful name and
delightful house—has a façade replete with architectural quips and quaintnesses, though, in the main, the
staircase outline to the sides of a building at the top
is far from being an idea of unchallengable beauty.

One memorable nook I wandered into by numerous, dark, narrow, ill-smelling passages, some over tiny bridges spanning one or other of Aalborg's pervading water-brooks. It was an aged courtyard, the bowed houses looking upon it black and venerable under the weight of their years. No whitewasher had been commissioned here. There were heavy, rotting wooden balconies to the windows, and aged crones with white mutches sat in them, telling ancient tales, and doing wool-work; and above, on the most suitable broad ridge to a roof that any bird could find in all Jutland, was a stork's nest, with a ragged old red-legged bird on one leg, his long red nose bent intimately towards one of the balconies, where two old dames were cornered. A vile telephone wire crossed the courtyard. Otherwise this was perfect—a reproduction of a spot of Aalborg life in the sixteenth century.

Down by the water-side, too, the town pleased the eye, and the high railway bridge to the west, over the opaline fiord (now calm and transfigured by the sunset radiance), was anything but a blot on the scene. I here met a British sailor or coal-heaver smoking a disconsolate solitary pipe among a heap of boards discharged from a ship that was not his. There was no doubting the man's birth country, and so I accosted him in English. But at the outset he was chary of confidences. I had to confess my nationality ere I won him over. Then, however, he was mine own as long as I pleased to treat him like a friend.

"I thought you was a blooming Dane," he said frankly, holding his pipe from his lips. "Some of 'em talks as well as we. But the idea of coming across a real Englishman in a hole like this!"

Impelled by a sense of duty, I drew his attention to divers of the graces of the place. Was he blind to the charm of the green hill, for instance, about two miles east of the port, and round the base of which the fiord waters lapped so caressingly? And did he ever see a cleaner maritime, and to some extent manufacturing, town? But he was no æsthete; a very Gallio in matters of the picturesque. All I could get out of him not in dispraise of poor Aalborg was this—

"There's a house one of my mates took me to t'other night where we had a 'booze' for threepence apiece. It didn't cost not a halfpenny more, and I tell you we was fair drunk when we left. And all for half a tanner!"

I wished my countryman "Good-night" after this. He did not seem at all a proper person to trouble with offers of hospitality, in howsoever modest a way.

The sunset colours lingered so persistently behind the suspension bridge that I yielded to the temptation to walk away into the western suburb of

the town.   Here I found houses of a vastly different
pattern to those in the old part—four-storied, of
smug new brick, and with a pleasant little garden to
each of them.   And by the water-side were bathing
shanties, whence ladies were stepping with moist
gowns on their arms.   It is the fashion, it seems, in
summer for the town to enjoy an evening dip in
the fiord.   And a right good fashion too, when you
can thus swim from crimson pool to crimson pool,
or lie floating in a broad patch of golden water just
cooling down from the warmth of an average midsummer day.

I saw more storks, and merry pigtailed little girls
playing at "touch" in the suburban thoroughfares, and came upon a slip of a park, with rules for
pedestrians and rules for riders ; and here and elsewhere about the town I fell in with many cyclists,
who seemed to be under the constraint of no rules.
But none of their cycles were fit to hold a mudguard
to my "Sunbeam"; no, not even the cycle of a
dapper young lady, with long hair streaming behind
her, who all but ran me down, and acted as if she
had no bell.

It was half-past ten when I returned to the hotel,
and went to bed without striking a match.

The accomplished head-waiter called me early in
the morning, as I had requested.   He let in the midsummer sunlight through the windows, brought me

coffee, and told me of his affairs, so that I was forced
to think the other guests of the hotel were fonder of
their beds than of the morning air. While I was still
shaking off the dreams of the past night, he related
(in such choice English too that I wondered) how he
had betrothed himself to the head chambermaid at
the Phœnix. "We shall," he continued, "be married
in August, and open a hotel of our own, and many
are the Herrs who have kindly promised us their
obliging favours and custom. There will be one fine
object about our hotel—it is to have a ball-room for
two hundred men and women. In Aalborg they are
fond of the dance when the weather is cold, and we
hope to make much money. I do not think I could
marry any one with better prospects than the head
chambermaid at the Phœnix, and the young lady
is of the same opinion." It seemed a sufficiently heartless alliance on both sides. However, he
and the young lady were the best judges of the requirements of their lives, and so I did not mention
the word "love," but congratulated him while I
yawned. Only then did he descend becomingly to
my own business.

"The smith Worsaae, my Herr, desires the hotel
porter to say that it will be eleven o'clock before the
cycle is ready."

So I could not be off to Randers as I had proposed. Maledictions on smith Worsaae!

For three bright hours I improved my acquaintance with Aalborg, having twice during the time looked in at the smith's factory. This consisted of but three lads, two sheds, and a diminutive yard. The lads were frank, sympathetic young Danes. Two of them watched the third patching my "Sunbeam's" tyre, and condoled with me while they complimented the cycle itself. They had not, they said, seen a more beautiful machine. One of them made me smile with a simile.

"It charms like a woman," he said. Nor did his comrades, both in their teens like himself, see anything precocious in the utterance of so Gallic, indeed Parisian, a sentiment.

I learnt to respect Aalborg for its shops. Booksellers especially are here much in excess of the average. I inquired if there was as eager a demand for English novels in the "Tauchnitz" as the shelves full of them seemed to imply. The tradesman assured me in answer, that he had many regular purchasers of the books—"English being greatly read by the Aalborg ladies." All honour to the ladies of this fair little town (though large for Denmark) for the honour they thus confer on my nation.

Eleven o'clock passed, and my "Sunbeam" was still on the stocks. One of the lads had tried it, and, in spite of his fellow-workman's warranty of soundness, it had again gone flat. Smith Worsaae himself was surprised. He came across from his shop with the works of a watch in his hand and a glass in his eye, on purpose to say so. But he and the three lads promised me, by their immortal souls, that I should be on the road at three o'clock.

That promise was fulfilled. Meanwhile I had dined on cold dishes at the hotel Beier, and, to give one more illustration of the singular cheapness of living in Denmark, I must tell how I dined. I ate smoked salmon, eel in aspic, pressed beef and tongue, cold veal, cucumber salad, cheese, bread-and-butter, and drank a bottle of Carlsberg beer, all for the sum of thirteen-pence halfpenny. Nor did I stint myself in any particular. The civility with which I was waited upon was of itself worth fully thirteen-pence halfpenny.

At three o'clock I departed from Aalborg, and took to the bridge of boats, sanguine, and rejoicing in the June sunshine. I was for Aaby again, to inquire if the little Metha had danced to her contentment on St. Hans' Day, and perchance I would be back in Aalborg ere nightfall, ready for Hobro at dawn the next day.

No high-road for me this little run. I meant to view the churches of Hvorup and Vadum, and so to get at Aaby without the constant accompaniment of whines from the wires of the telegraph.

Now Hvorup is on a hill, and its name, being interpreted, is "How up?" I reached the base of the hill by the Saeby road as far as that fatal milestone of the day before. Thence it was necessary to diverge through cornfields, the path a degraded score in the soil, which was sandy. The landscape towards Hvorup was green and treeless. The white church tower and the blue background of the heavens completed it as a picture. There were, however, larks enough overhead and in the fields, heralding with song my approach to the church.

But when I was near the top of the hill, having ridden where a week ago I should certainly have walked, I felt a pain somewhere. I was off and on the red earth in a moment. Alas! my "Sunbeam" was trailing a wounded limb as if I had not paid smith Worsaae three crowns for repairs, and given a gratuity to each of the boys. The pump was ineffectual. I pushed the poor thing into the churchyard and let it lie against the wall, while I sat on the church doorstep and pondered. Five miles to Aalborg and a rough ten to Aaby—which should I choose? I was still undetermined, when the inevitable churchyard lady appeared, in black all over, to open the door. But it was not for me. She pointed towards a farmstead in the south, whence I saw, without difficulty, a knot of persons with a black coffin in their midst. She also pointed to a prepared grave. I felt something like a mourner myself as I trundled my bedimmed "Sunbeam" down the slope towards another church tower, that of Vadum, two miles distant in the west. My state of mind was such that I craved sympathy and welcomes with quite a passionate craving. Besides, in my actual choleric under-current of mind, I could not answer for my tongue if I were to trundle straight back to smith Worsaae, five hot miles. I was therefore for Aaby and its *kro*, the hearty red-faced landlord, the little Metha, and the soothing garden with its mignonette and great old chestnut tree, the summit boughs bare and blasted, whereon the Aaby starlings loved to hold their parliament.

This decision was not hard to come at. But oh, the weariness of acting literally upon it! I was three energetic hours on this Jutland by-road, which zigzagged and circled so that it made the distance quite ten miles; and for roughness it was only to be classed with parts of the roads in the Ringkjöbing Amt. Vadum gave me a brief rest. But though the village was rather pretty, with some high trees about its houses, and the unwieldy lady of this churchyard left her spudding at the graves to talk to me without (she said so) the least design on my pocket, I could not give it its dues of admiration for thinking of what was yet before me.

I lost my way, and wandered off until I was on the

southern borders of the Great Wild Moor, and then I had to push back again across reedy meadows of immeasurable size, thick with cows, and not a few bulls. As for the denizens of this district, they seemed not half as intelligent as other Jutlanders. The little children took to their bare heels and ran from the stranger man, and their parents, at the first question put to them, said plump, "I do not understand," and gave themselves no pain in the attempt to understand. At Vester Haldne, having begged for milk, I did get water, which was something. But the woman who tendered the jug had such very red legs that I drank with less pleasure than you would have supposed. Her toes, too, were a bestial sight, for she had come straight from a dung-heap, where she had been looking, she said, for hens' eggs.

It was past eight o'clock when I tottered into the Aaby *kro*, taking them so much by surprise that for a time they could do little more than express their surprise with interjections. But they soon opened their amiable hearts in the old way, and, late though it was, Metha went to the strawberry bed, Herr Nielsen took the fork to dig new potatoes, while the large Fru left her dressmaking maidens (three of them, stitching at such a rate), and began a lively campaign among the pots and pans.

CHAPTER XIII

"Sunbeam" and I part company—An excursion to Öland—
The thousand-acre wood—By the Nibe Broad—Vesterby—Öxholm—The tombs of the Levetzau—The cold-
blooded *handelsmand*—Skittles and the pig-drover—A
tranquil evening.

I DID not see much of the little Metha this evening. She had a young friend with her from Aalborg
—a pale-faced maiden, who wore her frocks cut un-
beautifully low at the neck both in front and at the
nape, and the exactions of friendship were supreme.
The girl had come to the inn for the Sunday's dance
in the wood. She looked as if she had danced too
much, and was as different as a peach and a snow-
ball from my landlord's little daughter, whose cheeks
and eyes were aglow with the raptures induced by
loving companionship. I was formally—somewhat
too formally — introduced to her, while Metha
quivered with anxiety to see what happened. But
nothing very grave happened, and afterwards the
two damsels intertwined their arms, and went into
the garden to tumble each other about on the dewy

191

grass under the sympathetic presidency of the Fru.

That evening, before I went to bed, I saw an excellent mirage over the low-lying land between Aaby bridge and the north-west. It was when the kine in the great meadow by the old manor-house were making noisy pretence of being annoyed with the cowherds who were urging them towards their stalls. The western sky had done with its earlier sunset splendours; pallid crimson and saffron had succeeded the staring flame colours of half-past nine to ten o'clock. Then it was that, strolling with a cigar in the direction of the manor-house, I beheld an illusive vapour steal over the north-western horizon, and, rising from it, church towers and farmsteads, which were not there ere the vapour rose. I watched them come and watched them go; for still later the white mist thickened and swallowed up the eccentric vision it had created. Such spectacles are not rare in Jutland.

In the morning my landlord behaved nobly. He made my "Sunbeam's" sorrows his sorrows, and confided the machine to the Jetsmark carrier, who was to say strong sayings to smith Worsaae. Then, having ascertained that I longed to see the island of Öland, in the first westerly broad from the Lim Fiord, he said he found it exceedingly convenient to drive out to Bratskov, to interrogate a man about some pigs. Would I, he inquired, oblige him with my company?

And so, at ten o'clock or thereabouts, when he ought to have been getting in his last field of hay, behold him arrayed in his gala clothes, whip in hand, seated in a very solid cart, and scolding his Fru for not having thought of the Herr's dinner. This omission was soon remedied. Then I mounted beside him. "But hold!" quoth he, when about to drive off. He cried aloud for Metha. Had the child thought of some cigars for the Herr, and put them with the bread and meat and bottles of beer in the haversack? No; Metha had naturally thought of no such low masculine appetite. But she hastened to atone. The Havana cigars (with the Hamburg name on the box) were thrust into the cart, and we drove away, smiled on by the village of Aabybro and the blue heavens.

Truly it was a day of sunshine. This vast lowland district had never looked so fair as now under the bright cloudless sky. The farmers were all abroad in their grass-lands, and the tinkle of mowing machines joined chorus with the larks. The pair of us smoking Hamburg-Havana cigars, my landlord and I avowed that we felt mightily in accord with the weather.

The road was crowded with vehicles this day—carriers' carts, pig wains, milk vans, dilapidated chaises and such four-wheeled things as the Jutland aristocracy (or the nearest local approach to the equivalent of an aristocracy) are not ashamed to be seen in.

My landlord's boyish glee in saluting every one was quite inspiriting. I feel sure his Fru would not have liked to see him kiss his hand to so many women. He had, moreover, something loud to say to the majority. Only with two wayfarers did he show no sympathy, and these also, sad to tell, were women. I fear I shall lower my landlord in the general esteem when I confess that he put finger and thumb to his nose to these poor souls. They were certainly not abhorrent to the eye. But they were, he told me, a couple of deluded fanatics, who went about the country begging the people to drink no more beer, and to sign their names in a book to show that they meant to keep this ridiculous undertaking. They wore black, as became the apostles of such black principles, and walked with no more grace than you would expect in fanatic water-bibbers.

"I cannot help it," my good companion said to me in apology for his slight breach of manners, "I owe it to my trade."

Of course he did very wrong; but, on the other hand, I suppose even the best-natured of bishops, not having a private income, would not feel in perfect charity with the individual who made it his exclusive business to go from house to house canvassing the downthrow of the episcopacy.

At the temperance inn of Langeslund we paused to drink milk. I rather think this was a jest on my landlord's part. Milk—he! But so it was. The non-intoxicating landlady served us with two tall tumblers of unrivalled milk and very little speech. My landlord winked at me, and tossed the fine fluid down his brandied throat. I insulted him terribly the next moment by attempting to pay for the milk.

We kept the Aggersund high-road for about nine miles, and then turned south until we came to the little village of Öxeby on the water-side, with the cool woods of Öland just across the Sound. But it was plain here how very narrowly Öland has escaped belonging to the mainland. As a matter of fact, the tide being low, there were only about twenty feet of salt water left in the channel; the rest of the half-mile was given up to mud and rich meadow-land that had grown out of the mud, and was yellow with buttercups. Anciently there must have been more water, or else the legend of an important naval battle here in long-past times receives a certain discredit. But the mud is excellent mud. A number of cows stood pensively knee-deep in it, and some forty years ago a man wading through it, before the present causeway was constructed, slipped his toes into something, which was found to be a heavy gold ring large enough to encircle his ankle.

We had a few words with the Öxeby *handcls-mand*, and then drove gallantly across the bridge into the first bit of primitive forest I had met with in Jutland. Very winsome it was too, of beech, oak, and birch, with such undergrowth of bracken as tempted the feet to stray into it. And when we had gone a mile in these sylvan shades, we came to a clearing between some especially fine hills, and a medley of boards, barrels, and trestles, amid which was a wooden sign tablet bearing my landlord's name and place. A romantic spot, if ever there was one !

This was where they had danced on St. Hans' Day up to midnight or thereabouts, and here for centuries earlier also, I doubt not, the local Danes celebrated their mysterious and less mysterious revels. But to-day all was tranquil. The sunlight threaded through the tree-tops, and made a lacework of radiance on the smooth sward. My landlord and I had the wood to ourselves ; all Öland too, it seemed, for we had seen neither house nor human being since crossing the Sound.

And now, what must this estimable Jutlander do but propose that he should leave me, and on his own feet cover the hot distance between Öland and Bratskov—five severe miles. The cart was for me to drive about Öland in, just as I pleased. Only when I had seen enough of the wood and the church and town, might I, at my convenience, drive back and on to Bratskov, where my landlord would be awaiting me.

This was hospitality, according to the dim lights of the Aaby *kro*. And already the good man's face was wet with the heat, from the mere exertion of sitting in a cart. In Paradise itself I would desire the companionship of no better souls than such as Herr Nielsen's of the Aaby *kro*.

Not without much ado and persuasion was I permitted to stride on my way at random in Öland, with my luncheon haversack on my shoulders. So long as I stayed in this forest ball-room, so long did my landlord try his sternest to get me into the cart and the reins into my hand.

I soon fell in love with this little island in the Nibe Broad. Its wood was a very gem among woods. Even where it ended, on the margin of the water, it was still most beautiful. Here, however, I came upon cottages and strips of cultivated land, with barley and rye and potatoes between the green shade and the blue broad. Also, to my distress, and apparently hers, I came upon a comely damsel whom the heat and her spade had reduced to working among the potatoes in nothing but her shift from the waist upwards. The maiden dropped her implement at sight of me and ran to an elder tree, on which she had hung her rejected other garments.

Then, by a lane all overhung with dog-roses, with yellow iris crowding at the base of the hedges, and tall trees overshadowing the hedges, I wandered I cared not whither, confident that I should be guided by destiny to a suitable spot for my modest meal, which weighed heavy upon my shoulder. This I found in a break through the wood. There was an irregular grassy space on the fringe of the wood, with old thorn trees dotting it, and plump sheep huddled about under the trees, gasping as if the sun was at a duel *à mort* with them. By this pretty margin I crept into the wood again and discovered a gnarled tree trunk that served my purpose. And here, saving the flies, I made as gay a luncheon as a man could who was alone, and had eyes and thoughts only for the rural graces around him. Now and then a lamb bleated at me, and there was ever the song of the birds among the leaves and high over the trees. And the blue of the hot heavens glowed through the lattice of the tree-tops, and was as bright as the grass at my feet.

After this the devil possessed me, and incited me to do a foolish thing. I sauntered away and left the wood and reached a broad level of naked land, uncultivated, which ended only in mud and the waters of the Nibe Broad, with the island of Gjölland not much more than a mile distant; and here I lay down in the blazing sunshine and fell fast asleep. I had designed to bathe, but the mud was too repellent. And so I fell asleep instead, and awoke in an hour with divers pains that stayed with me all that day, nor left me until supper-time.

For all that, I would not be baulked of the rest of Öland. From this, the east side of the island, I made my way to Vesterby, or West Town, thankful at least that I had not the two bottles of beer on my back. The lane soon lost its first beauty. No more dog-roses, wild hops, jessamine and scentless violets; but just a low-trimmed hedge on either hand, and grain-fields beyond with a cluster of houses where the island ended in a tongue of mud. The glory of the thousand acres of forest was behind. Where the trees thinned somewhat to the west, with a singular ridge of green grass-land between me and them, I discerned the glitter of a weather-vane. The church to which this belonged was hidden, but I knew that beyond the ridge was the *kloster* attached to the manor-house of Öxholm, both of which, a small matter of seven centuries ago, were given up to the secluded sanctities of monastic existence.

The village of Vesterby was altogether the most model place of its kind I had seen in Jutland. Its houses were either of very clean red brick or stone, with new thatch of great thickness to every roof. But it was in the regard for details that I most admired these Ölanders. Every house had a neat short ladder hung on nails against its wall; to each house was a trim heap of squared peats, a well worked by two long poles in the tripod fashion, a pig or two in a clean sty, a certain number of bright flowers in a methodical garden, and three or four polished milk-cans standing full or empty by the back door. The island's name suggests milk, since it was probably called Öxholm before Öland, Öxholm meaning the island of oxen, and oxen presupposing the mothers of oxen. One thing more: to each house in its snug little brake of low shrubs belonged a drove of geese. It was these touchy rascals who told all Vesterby, that for once there was a person in their midst who was not even the postman, nor yet an itinerant *handelsmand*, nor the individual who collected the milk-cans, and trotted them off through the wood to the "milkery" at Öxeby.

From Vesterby it was much less than a mile to the manor-house. Looking back when I was half-way, I was impressed by the prettiness of Öland's chief village's situation, with the shining broad on both sides of its headland, and the lands beyond a weak purple against the strong blue of the heavens. I was also impressed by the queer look of so many men on the Vesterby roofs. If the villagers had not almost unanimously unhitched their respective ladders and set them to their walls, thus clambering to their respective vantage positions to regard this unquestionable wonder—a stranger!

I forget the name of the present lord of the manor of Öxholm. He is, however, a person of distinction. His house is most convincingly manorial, with its pretty turrets, its English garden, and the thickets of trees and flowering bushes therein. But I liked not the recurrence of the notice-board "Privat" about his premises, though that too gave only the more emphasis to his aristocratic position. The old and the new were tastefully blended in this dwelling-house, which must, however, be considered damp and doleful in the winter-time.

Hard adjacent to the manor-house was the monastery church, which immediately aroused esteem. For one thing, its roof and saddle were leaded, not of red tiles; also it had a famous high back. Its whiteness was ordinary, though it went well with the lavish verdure all about it, including the graves, which seemed preposterously numerous for so sparsely peopled an island, some being circular in form. Syringa and yellow and red roses bloomed in abundance over these Öland dead.

They were repairing the church. This enabled me to enter without guidance of any kind. It was

the tower that was at fault. So said the mason, who
went in and out of the aisle with his pipe in his
mouth and his hat on his head.

Now I ought here straightway to have been capti-
vated by the fine proportions of this Öxholm church,
with its high groined vaulting and shapely windows.
But all my attention was devoted instead to an
ancestral burial chapel the like of which I had not seen
in Jutland, though in Roskilde's cathedral, where
Denmark's kings lie, there are many such of far more
ornate pretensions. The chamber lay to the north of
the choir, and held four huge marble monuments as
well as a fair number of silver coffin-plates nailed to the
walls. Hereunder repose the heads of the Levetzau
family, who for the seventeenth and eighteenth centuries at least held lordship in Öland. Their titles
were recounted with true epitaphal unction, and so
were their virtues. But the best of these relics of
dead greatness was outside the chapel by the altar.
The "high and mighty and well-born Herre Hans
Friderich Levetzau, knight, counsellor of his Majesty
the King of Denmark and Norway, and Lieutenant-
General" besides, here stands in marble. His
mightiness's left gloved hand is set in his side, and
with his other holding a gilded baton, he strikes the
regal silly attitude that one associates with Louis
Quatorze—a swollen starched effigy in white marble.
With him is his "exalted and well-born wife, Fru

Lucie Emerence Brocktorf." Her ladyship is fully
as theatrical as her spouse. She holds a Bible and
a skull in one hand, while with the graceful finger-
tips of her other hand she touches her low-cut lace
corset.

Such grotesques in defiance of death are of course
common enough with us, who have Westminster
Abbey and St. Paul's open every day of the year.
But to the simple plebeian Jutlander, who has never
seen a lord, and has to rely on outside information
for details of a lord's make-up, these Levetzau
statues must be quite affectingly instructive. The
villagers of Vesterby and Österby of Öland are very
blessed in their privileges. It is odd if they are
more than a quarter as republican at heart as the
rest of Jutland. No matter if there is just nothing at
all beneath these marble excrescences but dust and
rotten bones, as powdery and brittle as any under the
lowliest heap in the churchyard. They do not see
the parody of pomp, the screaming farce of human
greatness in life, let alone in death. Their highness
and mightiness Hans Friderich and Lucie Emerence
are every seventh day a sermon in stone more com-
municative, I warrant, than the pastor's words. Every
village in every land ought, methinks, to have its
saint under a turf mound in the churchyard, to
counteract the insidious influence of these marble
abortions in the church; and while to the flamboyant

figure on its pedestal in the choir, where the little village boys can best see and wonder at it, a yard-long scroll of virtues may be allowed, let the saint among the worms lie nameless.

I am afraid one of the men with a hod of mortar on his shoulder is responsible for this little attack of flatulency. He took off his hat before the monument of Hans Friderich, having kept it on while he trod over the ashes of several other dead in the middle of the aisle. He came to me to murmur about the amazing nobility and importance of the earlier lords of Öxholm.

"There are none like them now," he said ruminantly.

"The megatherium also is no more," said I. I could not refrain, but I hope I said it with befitting sadness. "Why," I proceeded, for he stared, "are there so many 'private' boards about the manor-house gardens?"

Whereupon he gave up even staring, but turned, and, with his hat clapped on his thick head again, carried his mortar down the aisle and up the tower. He and his work, honest fellow, are, I imagine, well suited.

It was far better in the grand old wood of Öland than in the precincts of Öxholm. I now entered it from the south side, so that when I came forth at Öxeby I had traversed it triangularly. Here was

a gamekeeper's cottage with yelping dogs in their
kennels behind, and here, too, were more notices,
forbidding intrusion upon the forest peace. But
in spite of them I roamed among the beeches and
pines at my leisure, and, thus wading through the
undergrowth of juniper, bracken, and the softest of
grass, reached the lane again near the Sound.

The name of Öland merits fame throughout Jutland for this thousand-acre wood. Every young town
in the country aspiring to possess a *skov* of its
own, should first send a deputation to this little
island. Having studied the natural wood here at its
best, they should then model their baby plantations
upon it.

The day was still very hot when I came upon the
Aaby road in quest of my landlord. We had arranged
a tryst; but it was no great matter that he was half
an hour behind time. I found sport enough by the
roadside, smoking the Hamburg-Havana cigars and
scenting the hay all around me. When my good friend
did appear it was plain he had been hospitably
entertained at Bratskov. Well he deserved it too.
But I thought it advisable to take the reins, having
heretofore had no experience of the Jutland medical
men and desiring none. At six o'clock we reached
the inn, I on my part surfeited with pleasure, though
this was a little adulterated with well-merited pain.

They had been hard at work at the inn all the

time of our absence : the Fru and her sewing-girls in one room, Metha and her young friend at the bar, and the maids in the kitchen. So we were told. Furthermore, at the door was a dapper gig which the ostler was washing down. With the gig's owner I was confronted unexpectedly when I went up-stairs to my room. If they had not made him free of the apartment, and if he had not stretched himself out on my bed and seemingly throttled himself with a very large feather mattress, which covered him from his neck to his heels! He made rattling noises, so that I awoke him, not knowing if he were near his end or merely playing the pipe in his wonted way. Then, with apologies, he sat up and explained. He had been travelling all the night or nearly ("piece goods"), and had another nocturnal journey before him. The gudewife had said he might go to sleep up-stairs for three hours, and he had accepted her invitation. Would I excuse ?

Of course I excused, and left the poor man to finish his sudorific slumber. A burning midsummer day, my room with a south aspect, and yet this Jutland *handelsmand* must have a feather-bed equal to five blankets atop of him and all his clothes ere he can lie in comfort !

Afterwards I played a mild game of skittles with a pig-drover, who said he meant to keep where there was shade until the evening had spent itself.

"The night's the season for pigs this time of the year," he said, and I cordially agreed with him. Homicide were an offence far inferior in the punitive scale to that of the drover who penned his pigs at an inn for the night instead of urging them on to slaughter under the silvery stars.

This drover wore a very bright blue necktie, and smoked a three-foot pipe. All the same, he was an easy victim at skittles. He asked me if I belonged to Hjörring, whereat I smothered a blush. Either they must be very fair skittle-players at Hjörring, or else their accent is of the kind to make Holberg rise in his grave and forbid any mother's son of them to enjoy education at his famous college of Sorö—the Eton of Denmark.

Somehow—it may be fancy—it seemed to me that I sank in Metha's esteem from the time of this game of skittles. Certain it is that she opened her large eyes very wide when she caught us thus engaged. She was bearing a *bock* for the drover, and spilled some of it.

"Have you," she said to me, "seen Elise?"—her young friend.

I had not seen Elise.

"There is no one with her," Metha continued, casting at the drover a look of such scorn as I should never have supposed could have been raised in such eyes. The man of pigs took a deep draught and fidgeted. Any one under the circumstances would have done the same, or worse. I was sorry for him.

"Well, we must finish our game," I remarked. What if Elise was alone? I judged no one would be likely to eat her, and Denmark is not Spain, where, in some parts, it is still supposed to be an eternal disgrace for the gently-nurtured maiden to be out of doors unattended by a hag. But, with a toss of that absurd small head of hers, Metha, the landlord's daughter, flung herself off. After that I felt but little pride in my triumph over the pig-drover.

From him I parted company, and meandered by the banks of the river Rye, where it runs south of the bridge. Herr Nielsen's hay-land was in this direction, but I never reached it. The riparian barley was full seven feet high, and, though fair with poppies and cornflowers, discomfited with its stalks. There had been tales told me of the large fish in the river, including salmon. The river Rye, however, is as thick with alluvial matter as most other streams in Jutland, and I believe the tale of salmon to be a myth. Nor had they served me anything the least like fish at the table of the Aaby inn. Yet it is not an ugly river, and I might have killed the hour previous to supper in a worse fashion than thus wandering aimlessly along its soft crumbling margin.

Supper was not half so gay a meal as it ought to have been. There were no strawberries and cream, and though Metha attended on me (with a silver ring on one of her stubby fingers), my imperfections still lay heavy on her soul. She again mentioned Elise, this time to inform me that as soon as she had served me with coffee she was going to take her friend a walk along the Aalborg road, whence they proposed to deviate by the first turning to the left after passing the church. " Not," she added, with a pretty pout, " that we desire any one to accompany us, for we have always much to say when we are together."

Thereafter, in the gloaming of my inn chamber, and piqued by the pains which I ascribed to my imprudent siesta in broad sun-glare on the Öland mud bank, I smoked sadly and moralized as I had moralized earlier in the day, also subsequent to that foolish freak. I assured myself solemnly that it is always unwise to attempt to return on the trail of former pleasures. Time effaces such footmarks infallibly. In life's jaunt it is well ever to tread new ground. Whether this yields rapture or not, it is a mere toss-up, as at first. To each hour its individual potentialities; and there can be no postulating about the future.

I am afraid I must have dozed—and no wonder—upon such meditations. It was quite dusk, save in the west, when I roused myself, and hurried away with all despatch for the first turning on the left

P

from the Aalborg road past the Aaby church. The
evening had waned superbly into night. The white
mist was again over the green meadows, and the
smell of cut hay was predominant over the other
many perfumes of these Jutland lowlands. Voices
sounded pleasantly from the village, and passers-by
wished me "*God aften*" with brisk hilariousness.
Some one had got into the Aaby belfry and was
trifling with the bells. Their music drifted through
the cool air and across the snowy vapour that veiled
meadows, cornfields, and moor. But I must have
been too late. I saw no trace of that exacting young
damsel and her friend, and in the end moved
stealthily back to the inn and my bed.

CHAPTER XIV

The last of Aaby—A drive to Aalborg—The desperate lover—
On the road to Hobro—The wood of Rold—A Danish
pastor—Hobro—An evening ride, ending badly—Mariager.

AND now it was "farewell" for ever to the Aaby
inn, its inspiriting tumult and its cool garden with
the gregarious starlings on the topmost tree stumps.
I had come to it, not knowing what might transpire
in it; it had yielded many soothing hours and
minutes of exultation; I had even forgotten my
"Sunbeam" under the halo of its pleasures, and was
content thus to forget it.

There was a choice of ways of returning to
Aalborg and smith Worsaae, for whom I had sought
some effective words in my pocket dictionary of
Leipzig. I might walk, or I might ride in the
Jetsmark cart. But neither was my fate. Of all
things, they were, said Herr Nielsen, short of cheese
at the Aaby inn; besides, Elise was to be sent back
to her doting family in Aalborg. "They love her
very much, and cannot spare her for more than three
days at a time," Metha informed me. Hence the

Aaby vehicle was again to be requisitioned, and it was assumed, as a matter of course, that I should go in it.

My second bill here was more surprising than the first. I had lived the better part of two long days at the inn, eaten two dinners, with other meals, drunk no one knew (or cared, it seemed) how much soda-water and cognac, how many intercalary cups of coffee, also with cognac, or how many bottles of the Carlsberg beer, and smoked perhaps fifteen Hamburg-Havana cigars, and was asked to pay six crowns, or six shillings and ninepence.

"That is a mistake," I retorted, when Metha defiantly told me the total.

"It is no mistake," she said, with answering defiance.

"But it is too little," I urged.

"It is not too little. And where, please, is my poem book?"

The poem book was on the table. At request I had written something in it—two lines of Danish that rhymed, I hope, and were meant to be helpful along the thorny yet advisable paths of virtue. She read them, did not jeer, indeed hurried from the room, to return shortly with words to the effect that if I did not pay six crowns, I should pay nothing at all. The Öland drive was an affair of friendship, not crowns. She wondered I could think otherwise.

There was not over and above enough room in the cart for Elise and me, when the Aaby ostler and

Fru Nielsen were added to the company. The Fru was such a spectacle. I do not know with how many cubic feet of parti-coloured bonnets she had tormented her poor head on this hot day; but I do know that if she had not clothed herself in other parts with equal abundance, she would have reeled over the side of the cart from top-heaviness. Furthermore, though she wore her hands gloveless, there were five rings on her ten fingers. She was also resplendent in gold chains and a brooch that shone like a sun. Clap a shot-purple parasol over her rubicund face, which soon melted with the combined heat of the weather and her garments, and you have Fru Nielsen to the life.

Elise was slim and white, with a straw nothing on her head, and primrose-coloured gloves. A contrast that ought to have bowed the Fru down to the floor of the cart, but rather seemed to heighten her in her innocent esteem.

It was a tedious drive, for the dust and the sluggish humour of the horse. But we had the Lim Fiord, gradually getting nearer on the south, miles of cut hay, farmsteads, villages, and millions of telegraph posts by the road-side to enliven us. Also, our conversation, in which the ostler, having given reins to the horse, took cordial part, with a three-quarter turn from his box towards us, and a cigar in the corner of his mouth.

Until now I had not known Elise. She was a girl of some culture, read books regularly at home, and, though so pale, with a cordial appreciation of a romp in the country.

"It was," she said to me softly one moment, when the Fru was excitedly arguing with the ostler about some grass-mark in the neighbourhood, "it was so nice in the garden last night. We were there till eleven. You did not come. My feet were wet when I went up-stairs."

Towards noon we reached Nörre Sundby, and alighted at the house of a friend. I was for saluting and going my way. Nothing of the kind was permitted, however, until we had all eaten straw-berries and cream, and drunk milk in the friend's house. Then, with hand-shakes and compliments, we parted.

Perhaps fortunately, smith Worsaae was out when I entered his shop. His boys, however, were at work, singing and smiling. Their happy looks disarmed me, and I was won by their assurances that my "Sunbeam" should be at the Nord that afternoon. The thing was being more thoroughly overhauled than any machine in Denmark had yet been. They meant me to have no more trouble with it.

At the Nord I found the old company. We dined agreeably, and afterwards the landlord and another proposed that I should go with them for a walk to the Aalborg *skov*. But I declined that walk. Its purpose seemed to me too grisly for anything. The facts were these. A week back a young merchant, who had given his heart passionately to an Aalborg damsel, came to the hotel, and made no secret about his intention of either gaining a wife or snapping his fingers contemptuously at the sisters three who weave the woof of human lives. For two days he was sanguine; then he fell serious, and wore a clouded countenance. It was conjectured that he was refused. And the next day he disappeared, and since then had not been seen or heard of. His luggage stayed unheeded at the hotel.

"In my opinion," said the landlord, shaking his head with the energy of conviction, "the man has hanged himself from an oak tree."

The walk to the *skov* was in search of the particular oak tree he might have favoured.

"The weather is so charming," the landlord added, to persuade me. He had an enviable cane with a gold head.

But I remained unpersuaded, and strolled away by myself to the bridge of boats, which offered more true exhilaration than a strangled lover swaying from an oak tree.

They did not, however, find the corpse; the

disappointment was a large topic at the supper-table. Nor had they learned aught about him or it (as it might be) when I rode out of Aalborg the next day, somewhere between one and two o'clock.

In the meantime the smith Worsaae and I had about three battles. I reserved fire until I could hold it back no longer, and then, I believe, I riddled him with bullets. One thing is sure—eventually he laid aside all the clocks and watches and barometers he was repairing, and gave himself body and soul to the supervision of my "Sunbeam," which I saw thrice in a most melancholy state of dissolution. Even with that the day waned, and I was still no nearer being on the road. And at bed-time the cycle was in the factory, with the three merry boys chanting catches over it.

It was the same the next day also, when the wind had turned south (an irritating circumstance), and I was tolerably sick of the St. John's Street that led to the back yard in which smith Worsaae's smithy lay hid from the eye of the town. But little by little hope now grew strong, and at noon my "Sunbeam" was given to me reconstituted. One of the boys, Hans by name, said with enthusiasm—

"Sir, you will be in Hobro on it in two hours. You will now move like steam."

Hobro is twenty-seven miles from Aalborg.

"May it be so," I answered, with sufficient frigidity.

There was an Englishman at dinner at the Nord this day. He really was concerned with butter, and the others hailed him accordingly. They could understand a man like him. He was an agreeable fellow, and, having viewed my "Sunbeam," he said that in all his future visits to Jutland he too would bring a cycle. The Jutland trains put him out of humour with the country, in spite of the immensity of its importance as a butter market.

I turned my back on Aalborg with extraordinary eagerness, trundled southwards up flagged streets till we were at a good height, and then, near the town wood in which the love-lorn merchant was supposed to have hanged himself, mounted and made a brisk descent into the country, with the railway closely parallel on the left. Words cannot tell how glad I was again to be on my limber steed, apparently restored to a prime condition of health. Only the wind was against the enjoyment of the afternoon, and that was not too assertive.

The road was very good, as became the main thoroughfare between north and south Jutland. But it was anything rather than level. A succession of hills indeed, which increased alarmingly in magnitude as we left Aalborg farther behind, and by Buderup-holm attained real loftiness. Ere then we had run through yet another Svenstrup, with no points about it, and called briefly at Ellitshöi, seduced by the mediæval look of the old King's Arms posthouse. It is not so very long since Jutland was untroubled by railways. Her stage-coach inns have not therefore had time for moss and rust like ours. The stabling to these old houses of entertainment on the Hobro road were well worth inspection. A penny bottle of soda-water franked me over the premises.

By Buderupholm, half-way to Hobro, the country changed much. Here I was some hundred feet above sea-level and could see very large patches of forest on the hill slopes before me. But I was not at all prepared for the fine valley of Gravle, into which a descent had to be made ere the woods could be traversed. This valley, or rather vale, with Gravle's red-saddled church commanding it from the heights, would be reckoned pretty even in Devonshire, with its heathy slopes and wooded crests, not to mention the pellucid trout stream which flows through it, and over which I ran by a road mended with nasty chalk flints. As for the farmsteads here, they were models in their neatness and the mellowed colours of their brick-work and thatched roofs. But it was nothing less than a mad pelt from Gravle to the bridge, with gradients which in England would, I think, be honoured by a post of warning from the Cyclists' Union.

This day I met not a few Danish cyclists on tour, in pith helmets, and with a spruce appearance that ought to have humbled me. But they were all very civil persons, and even when careering down a hill took the trouble to touch or lift their caps in salutation. They were also a good deal more warm than I, for the day was worthy of the season, and they had not the breeze in their faces to cool them.

Out of the Gravle dale the ascent was long and engaging. We were here on the hem of the wood of Rold, with which I was soon infatuated. This was quite another kind of wood to Öland's. The trees here were mainly magnificent Norwegian pines, though with copses of great beeches interjacent and glens with bright reedy pools, about which the silver birch hung its pretty tassels. These pines give character to the Rold wood. Superb fellows, with endless vistas between their symmetrical trunks, and magpies flitting among their glossy green twigs. For about three miles the road lifted and fell in this wood, and it seemed to me that thenceforward for ever I should be bound to maintain, against all comers, that there is nothing on our globe's surface more beautiful than a Danish forest. In midwinter these pines are as lovely as in midsummer: never more lovely indeed than when they are plastered with snow, save where the ice-diamonds deck them and glisten to the moonshine. Go a sledging in Norway in January, if you wish to value aright such a forest as this of Rold; and be abroad in the white and green groves when you have no lamps to guide you except the white shapes of the trees and the stars that seem set on their still summits. There is no forgetting the pines of Norway after such an experience. They are a joy firmly enshrined in the heart.

But the wood of Rold ended at length, and Rold village and red-saddled church appeared. Also the Rold *kro*, which was welcome, for I had now run twenty miles, many of them "coarse," and the flies were troublesome, even as the sun was hot.

To me in the Rold *kro* came the pastor of the parish, quick to discuss the many good qualities of my "Sunbeam," which he had, I believe, espied from his parsonage, and come forth to see, attracted by the sun-glare on it. He too was a cyclist. That he well might have been, but I should never have taken him for a priest. He wore a Scotch tweed suit like myself, an imperial beard, and a valuable topaz in his neck-cloth. His pipe signified nothing. Nor was his conversation at all of the ecclesiastical kind, while his drink was bottled beer. Upon the whole, methinks, the Danish clergy have a sufficiently easy life. They do not act as if they were elevated by their consecration above their fellow-men, and they certainly are not worn out by a superabundance of clerical work. Centres of culture in the moorland wastes and the forest wilds they may be, and doubtless often are ; and they marry like other men, and leave plenty of children to bear their names down through the ages of futurity. What if they are poorly paid : passing rich on a hundred a year? Money goes a long way in rural Denmark, and most of their pleasures are of the kind that money alone cannot buy—pleasures contingent upon their circumstances and calling. All which, to do justice to the youthful Dane in search of a career, he is well able to perceive. Some of my best-remembered hours as a vagabond at large have been spent as a guest in a Danish pastor's house, where the pastoress was young and lovely, the table excellent, the conversation and the library quite cosmopolitan. The vicar of Rold was just such a contented, philosophic man of God as the majority of his brother vicars : but from the way he cast beer down his throat, I hardly expect ever to hear of him as a bishop.

The remaining eight or nine good miles to Hobro were not remarkable. I had a succession of dismal *bakker* or ridge-like hills to scale. From their summits I saw much barley land and much moor. Viking tombs also reappeared. But the small pools in the black peat moor were oftentimes the brightest objects in the extensive landscape, with the white cotton-flowers quivering in the breeze on their brink, and the cloud shapes mirrored in their midst.

Five o'clock, however, found me on the steep edge

of the basin in which Hobro lies, happily clustered about the head of the Mariager Fiord. Here was the usual *skov*, and a fine one too. But the gradient through it was extremely severe and the road damp, thanks to the dense leafage on every hand, so that I had to give all my attention to the work I was engaged in.

Hobro is red-roofed. It has as many houses as you would expect in a town of about three thousand inhabitants, and nothing like as much bustle as its situation on a navigable water-way to the Cattegat would seem to require of it. But I was taken by its cleanliness, and in high spirits because smith Worsaae had finally done his duty to my " Sunbeam " in so exemplary a manner.

At the Hobro hotel I drank tea and answered a few inquiries. Neither the landlord nor his young waiter were used to tourists. That perhaps is why they charged me a crown for my refreshment, which was worth much less. This was the only place, except one other, in which there was the smallest suspicion of extortion on my purse during this cycle jaunt. And I owe it to the young waiter to add that, while subsequently preparing my " Sunbeam " for its eight miles in the cool of the evening, he offered a mild apology for his master's conduct.

Now Mariager is on the same fiord as Hobro, but nearer the sea. I was given to understand that the road was very good, nor was there any missing the way. I reckoned, therefore, that one hour would be ample time to allow for the run. As the evening was a singularly beautiful one, I looked forward to the little journey quite as much as to the famous old monastic home where I was to sleep for the night.

It behoved us to clamber out of Hobro by a gradient as steep as that which had brought us into the town, past a venerable suburb with archaic inns for the country folk and many pretty groups of people at their thresholds. Then, on the bare uplands again, though with something of the freshness of the sea in the air, my " Sunbeam " carried me gallantly about three miles to Skjellerup, where there is a church and little else. Another mile, and then, of a sudden, disaster came. It was the old evil—my " Sunbeam's " tyre was once more a cripple, and I a pedestrian. Smith Worsaae was a traitor to his craft.

The alternative before me was this—either to walk back to Hobro or to walk on to Mariager : a four-mile trundle in each case. Mariager won the day. But I achieved that walk in a state of mind not at all accordant with the golden tranquillity of the evening. Birds sang and coquetted in the hedgerows, plough-boys whistled with their teams in the reddish fields, and the waning sun transfigured the acres of ripening corn through which I passed. But I am ashamed to say smith Worsaae was in my mind, and the shadow of that miscreant "reparationist" blackened the beauteous face of nature.

It was eight o'clock when we reached a parting in the uplands, with one red church roof in the hollow, and wooded slopes leading to it. The still fiord shone yet farther below, and beyond it were the purpled hills of the other shore. I had seen no place in Jutland to equal this for beauty. Nevertheless, it was with a heavy heart that I pushed my poor maltreated "Sunbeam" down through the beech-woods into the silent red little town.

CHAPTER XV

THE entrance into Mariager was by a green arch of polled trees, which continued along the street side like a *boulevard*, and gave extraordinary grace to the neat little houses on either hand. I was indeed so smitten by the look of the town that I narrowly escaped entering off-hand the large "landsman's hotel," against which I had been warned (for insectile and other propensities) by the Hobro waiter. It was a surprisingly picturesque hostelry, with its half-timber work, tumble-down yard premises, and the ancient vehicles that cumbered its stones. Something, however, stayed me in time. This was nothing less than an infuriated Dane. The man must have quaffed too much corn brandy, or exposed his head overmuch to the sun. There he stood in the porch of the yard, with rough hair

Q

and a wry mouth, snapping his fingers at all
and sundry, and exclaiming rude things. Certain
kindly or inquiring women were on the far side of
the road, right in the focus of his gesticulations.
They exchanged sympathetic looks and nods, but
said nothing. If anything could have soothed the
raving man, the silence of his townswomen, their
clean blue gowns and compassionating faces ought
to have done the trick.

My haven for the night was quite a different sort
of house. The placidity of the grave ruled in it,
and only when I had knocked chairs and the floor
together, and roamed into many chambers—all, like
the inn itself, of one storey—did I procure the
attention of its handmaiden. Thereafter all went
well. I supped on cold slices, with strawberries and
cream, and took coffee in an arbour of the garden,
which, by its beauty, put even that of Aaby in the
shade. The landlord had the manners of a gentleman. He made my "Sunbeam's" misfortune his
own, and though I tried to dissuade him he went for
the local blacksmith, who, he thought, might at a
pinch be able successfully to turn his mind from
horse-shoes to the mechanism of a cycle tyre. There
is no certificated cycle smith in Mariager. This
alone says more about its seclusion and old-fashioned
ways than aught else.

But what a garden was this! Seen under the

gold of the sunset sky, with the quiet songs of birds
in its higher trees, and the shining of the fiord
through the brake of rose-bushes and syringa on
one side, it enchanted. It held so perfumed an air
too that I was fain to lay aside my cigar and breathe
it and nought besides. And from its sweet confusion of flowers and fruit trees (the cherries ripe for
picking) I had but to stroll into a smooth meadow,
with the hay set in loose heaps, to have the fiord
right before me, all crimson and gold like the sky,
and the farther hills with glorified wisps of cloud
lying along their summits. Hence I heard all the
human sound Mariager could evoke on this serene
beautiful June evening—the laughter of some boys
far out on the water, and the intermittent dipping of
their oars. A solemn stork stood erect on the edge
of his nest on a red cottage gable, and seemed
solemnly vain of the fine figure he cut thus cameoed
against the refulgent heavens.

It was nigh ten o'clock when I set out for a short
walk through and round the town. The dew was
cooling the air, and intensified the odour of cut grass
and blossoms which hung in the pent place. I came
to a baby pier in the water. On the fiord side of
its shed were a loving couple absorbed, as behoved
them, in each other. Then across the meadows,
careless of wet feet, with the western gold still
dazzling to the eyes. Here, in the middle of the

grass, sat an artist struggling with Nature at her
hardest. He plied his weapons right manfully, but
it must have been a losing battle. And so round by
lanes between red and white villas almost suffocated
by the sweetness and plenitude of flowering trees
and shrubs, and home to my inn.

Yet even now it was impossible to leave this
heavenly sky and shut myself into a room with a
bed. Eleven o'clock saw me still in the garden,
having assented to my landlord's request that I
would lock up the house. A quarter of a moon had
come up from behind the green hilly headland which
binds Mariager to the west; but the sunset had not
nearly exhausted its wealth of colouring. The fiord
was pale crimson near the meadows, pale purple and
silver further out; and the northern hills were so
finely limned against the roseate sky that I detected
a viking pimple on a ridge where before I had
marked nothing in particular.

Long shall I remember this night at Mariager on
the fiord of that ilk. If I had seen no other spot in
Jutland but this, I should record Jutland's praises
with absurd extravagance.

At five o'clock the next morning, the Mariager
blacksmith came and inspected my "Sunbeam." So
I was told, for my blinds did not come up until
seven, though those of the tailor and his wife in the
opposite house (both of us on the ground level) were

not pulled down at all. And at half-past five he went off, baffled, to his horse-shoes.

"He did not dare touch it for its beauty," said my landlord, when he brought me coffee into the garden at half-past seven. I plucked dewy cherries to my breakfast. There were also, of course, strawberries, in a silver bowl.

"And there is no one in Mariager competent to mend such a machine?" I asked.

The good man shrugged his shoulders. It went against the grain thus formally to condemn his native place.

Well, it could not be helped. The run of thirteen miles and a half to Randers would have to be a walk instead of a run. But the sky gave such promise of heat as to ensure me much warmth during that walk.

Ere leaving this pleasant nest, in which I would be content to live for ever if all the year could be June, I viewed the town. There was a leafy arch out of it in the east as at the entrance from the west, and an alluring road which ascended sharply, and then slid off into the woods, with a windmill on the hill-top well over the woods. By the water, which held a light veil over its repose, a Mariager youth with a long pipe in his mouth supported a maiden with his one hand while holding his pipe-bowl with the other. Nature here in the summer-time wars fiercely against the bachelor instinct. There can hardly be one unwedded man in the place. Lastly, I climbed to the church in the graveyard, where the plane trees had grown to a huge size. Here were many graves, over which the white church with its red roof and leaded conical tower, closely embraced by the high leafage, watched benignly. The wooded slopes close behind were aglow in the sunlight.

Of the Briggittine conventual house, founded in 1400 or so, a few fragments were discernible inside the lovely grounds adjacent to the church, now in the hands of a functionary. They were certainly not worth a ring at the functionary's bell, under his coat-of-arms, to view more narrowly. The church, however, promised better things. But it was locked, though with so crude a lock that I thought it no shame, and quite easy, to pick the lock. The grave-digger, commissioned for an interment in the afternoon, caught me at the business. He came to me with his mattock on his shoulder and his pipe in his mouth. The pipe somewhat hindered his smile, which nevertheless relieved me. He told me bluntly that he sympathized. The church was so fine a one that it ought, he said, to be open for all such "well-born gentlemen" as myself who wished to enter it. His grave was for a middle-aged woman. Trouble, he said, was at the bottom of her premature demise. Trouble in Mariager! Forsooth, then, we others ought always to keep our armour bright. But he was a civil grave-digger, and did not find it surpassingly ridiculous that I could hold high views of his town.

Within the church door I came first to a cluster of catholic statues; weak-kneed wooden saints and others, life-sized. They had been thrust ignominiously into a corner, and looked pitiable. Most unseemly of all were two gory Christs, one lying in a coffin. Either of these would even now fetch a certain number of crowns in Spain, where such properties fairly retain their value, if the towns be excluded. But Denmark has got long past that stage.

Whitewash is as much respected in Mariager as elsewhere in Jutland. But the spotless walls were, to some extent, made majestic by a studding of golden stars to the otherwise white ceiling. The loftiness of the church, and its vast sepulchral slabs set on end by the church walls, with skulls and cross-bones in strong relief on them, are now-a-days the chief testifiers to the building's earlier distinction. Its altar-piece also is uncommon, the Last Supper being wrought excellently in wood and varnished. The varnish seems a pity; but they have their own idea of artistic propriety in this land of the great Thorvaldsen.

It was nine o'clock when I started up the steep

road for Randers, pushing my poor "Sunbeam" before me. Overhead was such a sun as they get in Scandinavia in midsummer, to atone to them for the trials of midwinter. I did not like the task that was before me. Yet I meant, God willing, to be in Randers in time for the one o'clock dinner at the hotel Randers.

The shade of the beech trees in the wood was welcome, but not long enduring. In ten minutes I had climbed to the uplands, and Mariager, its leaded church tower and shining fiord, were lost wholly. I was among fields and moor—a shadeless land.

In the old days all this district teemed with people, we are told. The two fiords, that of Randers to the south and Mariager to the north, were, I suppose, accountable for such a population. But, save for the advantages they got from their proximity to the water, I do not think the ancient Jutes can be congratulated on their choice of a residence. They would have done far better in Kent or even Essex. Of course, however, I judged from inaccurate evidence. Gone now were the forests which presumably of old dignified these miles of rolling country. Once or twice, in the first six miles after the beech wood of Mariager, I did clash with a bent stripling of a wayside tree. Else all was naked and hot.

I rested briefly among the heather of a tomb pimple and trod underfoot the bits of pottery and bones a previous visitor had dug from the depths of the grave. Once, too, I dabbled my feet in a pond, a lovely lilied pond, with rushes to its borders, and a red farmhouse with a stork on it hard by. But in the main it was not pleasure, this walk of mine.

I grew to loathe my poor "Sunbeam," and to glance at it with disgust. Was I to push my ass all through Jutland in this humbling style? It had a stone of dead weight in its portmanteau, so that in all it represented a burden of something not far short of fifty pounds. And the angle of certain of the hills we had to climb was so stiff that I had to strive to keep even the flattened hind wheel rushing free of me and carrying the whole encumbrance right down into the valley. There were times when, if I had met a sagacious huckster, I would have sold him the thing for a five-pound-note, and given him my blessing for luck. With nothing to push, a stick in my hand, and another five-pound-note in my pocket, I should have felt a man again. As it was, I was a pedlar of the meanest kind, a man urging his goods across country in haste, and not resting by the roadside and tasting tobacco when the mood pleased. I could see no service in this back-aching pastime, except the improvement of what talent I possessed for the control of a perambulator. If it taught me nothing else, this melting forced march taught me to pity the average nursemaid. Yet she has smooth pavements for her smiling charges, whereas I had thirteen miles and a half of uneven roads.

At Gassum, a rude village with a red-saddled granite church, I begged some milk. But, as heretofore, the honest Jutlanders did not give milk. They had beer, which is esteemed far better, and it was beer or nothing. So said the little girl who tendered it brightly, and watched while I drank, her mother's voice instructing her from another room. Surely, I thought, so young a child as this will not be imbued with the Danish pride, which regards the donation of money for the donation of beer as an impertinence. But I was wrong. To see how the little maid bridled up!

"No," she cried, with hands uplifted as if I were a leper.

"Do," I pleaded.

"Nothing at all. I will not," she screamed, and ran from the room, clasping the empty jug.

Bless their sensitive hearts! But it is a pleasing trait on the whole. Though bitter, the beer carried me along to the next mile-stone with tolerable gaiety. These mile-stones were as large as the Danish mile is long. The latter is four and a half of our miles, and the Danish mile-stone is often an obelisk of stone from six to ten feet high, and the most conspicuous object in the landscape.

Well up above sea-level, I passed another Bjergby, or hill-town, and the final mile-stone. Thence into Randers the road broadened and coarsened, as all the Jutland roads do in the vicinity of a town. Also, the tendency was downwards. Glad, indeed, was I, at half-past twelve or so, to come to the first sprawling line of cottages which spelt the word suburb. The conventional steep descent and infamous paved way followed. Then I saw the fiord shine in the valley, and red houses, and what seemed to me a vast fleet of ships and steamers in the water. And so rejoiced was I, and proud of the pace at which I had urged my incubus, that, in a moment of laxity, I all but let the "Sunbeam" slip from my hands. A mad rush it would have made through the broad outer market-place, down into the paved heart of the town!

Some eight or ten extensive old inns in this market square (with a newish *skov* not far distant) witnessed strongly to the importance of Randers as a town. But the dinner-table at the hotel was even more vigorous in this respect. Here, when I had consigned my "Sunbeam" to the leading smith, I sat down to a long meal with eleven gentlemen, all of the commercial-travelling persuasion. They talked invoices, leather, timber, and other goods, as well as provisions, and perhaps not more than five of them were Germans. One who was next to me was so polite in his remarks and general conduct that I ventured to ask him where the Castle was. But it was a futile inquiry. The good fellow puzzled his head for a minute, and then tossed the question upon the table for the wisest of the others to grapple with. In the end it transpired that Randers the modern has kicked the castle of Randers the old entirely out of existence. Not a trace of it remains, though I imagine it stood where the borough wood now stands. Yet it was here that Niels Ebbesen the Brave, in 1340, on the first of April, having entered the town with a few Jutlanders as stout of heart and will as himself, caught Count Gerhard the Holsteiner and slew him, paving the way for a healthy reaction in the realm of Denmark, the expulsion of the tyrannizing foreigners, and a new and better king.

Five centuries and a half is a fair age for a town ; but in fact Randers was alive long before Niels Ebbesen. And its situation is such that it has no chance of doing aught but progress with the general progression of the country.

The Randers smith had sad things to tell about my poor " Sunbeam."

Still, I thought him an absurd pessimist when he

promised me the machine, safe and well, by three o'clock.

That left me barely half-an-hour to view the town, which has a museum and a red-brick church of great size, as well as many foul by-ways and alleys quite perfect in picturesqueness, with their bowed gables and carved black beams. The ships were of course nothing, though some of the coasting craft were quaint, big-bottomed things suggestive of many decades ago.

At three o'clock precisely I moved away with my cycle, sanguine (for the smith was an honest-spoken fellow), and anticipating with pleasure the run to Aarhus of one-and-twenty miles.

We crossed the long bridge, ascended the steep climb between fine trees by the broad Aarhus road, of which I had heard high praises, and then began the journey. But in one mile all was as it was before. Hope fled from me, and I trundled back to the town pervaded with woe.

After this the smith would say nothing until he had dissected my "Sunbeam." At the earliest I could not have my steed ere nightfall, though at the latest it should be ready by dawn the next day. In the end it was arranged that I should receive it at Aarhus by the first train in the morning. The smith would have sworn this on anything I liked to offer him for the purpose.

Then for two hours I breathed the air of the Randers streets. There were times when I was soaked in the mediæval, but it was with my handkerchief to my nose. However, in this respect Aalborg merits even more notoriety.

The journey to Aarhus was tedious, yet almost delightful. It cost three hours of time, but latterly the noble woods, having the snuggest of farmsteads set with their backs to the greenery, and the blue Brabrand lake, which we skirted for two or three miles, almost made up for the weary pace at which we moved. Here was beautiful Jutland, at any rate.

And so my fellow-travellers seemed to think. How they did revel in the glory of the midsummer evening! There were some school-boys in the car with me, singing and chattering and with their heads first at one window and then the other. And all along the train there was other singing. Once we passed a couple of dozen cattle trucks, crammed with excursionists, standing, and shunted. And the way they also sang, unmindful of their discomfort, taught me a lesson: old women and young men, and young women and grey-haired men all jammed together like hops in a pocket! Such bright little flower-gardens, too, as were the railway stations, with the crimson and black officials, and the tomato-coloured postmen, and either a bosky hill at the back of the station or a green meadow in front of it, with cows and a lustrous stream steal-ing through it, and the gala sunset sky over all.

I was tolerably charged with equanimity, in short, when, at about ten o'clock, we ran into Aarhus station. Yet had I had my "Sunbeam" I should have been in the city at six.

CHAPTER XVI

Aarhus Cathedral—The Ris wood—No cycle—Telephonic
remarks—Along the Cattegat shore—The Church of Our
Lady—An Aarhus music-hall—English talent.

AARHUS is the greatest town in Jutland, with
steamers every morning to Kallundborg in Zealand,
whence it is not difficult, aided by a little patience,
to reach Copenhagen by train.

The hotel Royal, to which I walked through wet
streets (for it had rained that evening), populous
with citizens and young folks affectionately inclined,
was quite perturbed with guests. They were flow-
ing in by two doors, ladies and gentlemen as well as
traders, whose swollen trunks made a mountain on
the omnibus top. Unaccompanied by my " Sunbeam," I felt a fraud, a man without standing :
neither a dealer in knickknacks, nor a person of landed
estate to whom a bed was merely a passing convenience until the carriage arrived in the morning.
But they are not psychologists at hotels, and, blind
to my depression, they received me here with a
courtesy that was perhaps incited a little by my

240

poor accent. A meal of cold slices, with beer, was served daintily in my own room, and the chamber-maid was nothing less than frivolous in her remarks as, at my request, she took away the superincumbent feather-bed and provided me with the woollen counterpane that always reminded me of my Esbjerg friend. And here I sat smoking and staring at the fat base of the cathedral spire outside until midnight chimed from the cathedral belfry.

There was a smart storm in the night. One clap of thunder seemed to have aroused every soul in the town; it was the talk of the place the next day. And heavens! how it did rain! I lay listening to the crash of it on the pavement, and watching the lightning, which was incredibly impetuous and blue. But, like all storms of all kinds, it passed, and the quietude of two o'clock in the morning ensued, with daylight already in the room.

Now as I could nohow get my cycle before ten o'clock, I thought nothing about it until that time. Aarhus did one good to see while I breakfasted in the café, in full view of the market square. The sun was bright and furbished up the dull red of the cathedral bricks. It also revelled in the gilt vane to the spire, which is not far short of four hundred feet above the square. This last was a mild tulip bed for colour. There was not quite enough red in

R

the show until you came to look into the baskets and barrows of the blue and white country folks. Then, however, the whole space seemed red, for every soul with anything to sell had brought strawberries into Aarhus. There must have been tons of the fruit on the cobbles. Its perfume swallowed that of the flowers, which also gave charm to the scene. But the hale brown faces of the people, and their smiling sprightliness, pleased me best of all.

From them I strolled into the cool cathedral. I went in by the south door, with a gigantic sepulchral slab handy for purposes of spiritual abasement. A very proper skeleton, some six feet high, was done in relief on the slab. It held a spade in the left paw and an hour-glass in the right, and grinned as skeletons will. But no one seemed to notice it, which assuredly must have touched even its ossified heart.

This vast church of red brick, with a score of chapels and more funereal tablets and effigies than I could count, is not to be described. I am not sure that it is worth detailed description. Even the Danish notables who lie behind the subtly-forged iron gates of the chapels and under its paving-stones would probably at this date prefer not to be mentioned. As for the many family portraits done on wood, with Dutch particularity, and mounted

against the brick columns and walls, they interested
more than they inspirited; and they did not even
interest overmuch, for they commemorated only so
many solid burghers, their wives and once-little ones,
all of whom had gone to dust about two or three
hundred years ago. The ladies, when they lived,
wore much clothing, while the gentlemen wore
clerical ruffs, flat hats, and clerical black. And that
is all that need be said about them.

The pendant ship of Aarhus Cathedral is as pretty
a model as any in Jutland. Moreover, it has a
history. Peter the Great bought it in Amsterdam,
and maybe meant to build a navy like it. But the
winds and the waves ruled otherwise, for they
wrecked the big ship which was taking this little
ship to his capital, and the little ship was taken
prisoner by the Jutlanders. Either Peter thought
the model not worth making a fuss about, or else his
Majesty of Denmark and Norway was too proud of
such a booty to let it go. Here it hangs in a side
aisle of Aarhus Cathedral, sways in the draughts
and gathers much dust.

The altar is the most engrossing article in the
place. It is almost too brightly agleam with gold
for a Protestant house of prayer; and the paintings
on it are of pre-Reformation times. But this latter
feature is only what one would expect. Our Lutheran friends blend their love of whitewash and

unadorned primness with a very genial tolerance of the grotesques and artistic graces of old Catholic imagery.

As a whole, Aarhus Cathedral is a noble building, in spite of its rather base material. Furnish its many white windows with stained glass like that of Rouen, and it would be a place of pilgrimage for the whole north.

This was my first visit to it. Ere I left Aarhus, I dare say I was in it five times.

Soon after ten I returned to the hotel for my "Sunbeam." Somehow I was prepared for the disappointment that met me. It had not come, and the next train for it was in the afternoon. Well, no great matter; at the worst I should have the more time in this city of near forty thousand inhabitants, and Silkeborg and Heaven's Hill, whither I wished to go for the night, were distant but two hours' run.

And so, to fill the morning, I made for the harbour, which had, for Denmark, a lively look, and walked by the Cattegat shore until I came to the Ris skov, of which Aarhus might well make a fair brag. The ticket "strawberries and cream" was in a surprising number of little shops by the way. One shop was a cobbler's, and his price for the luxury was threepence. Also they cried the fruit lustily in the streets of the old town, where the houses are of half timber and brick, heavily covered with primrose and white wash.

It was a placid day, hazy with heat over the water. The wood of Ris was therefore a great joy when I came to it. The seaward side of it is a white cliff, with little paths torn in it; but from the very brink of the cliff-top, and for hundreds of acres (I hope I am not too generous in my estimate) inland and along the shore, you have a dense forest of beech trees, with ravines here and there, and water brooks with rustic bridges over. Of course winding tracks abound, and there are many seats. And in the heart of it you have a café with little bowers under the trees, and tables and chairs.

The café might have been dispensed with, though I found it useful. But otherwise this wood of Ris won the heart completely. Civilization has worked better in some respects in Denmark than with us, and most conspicuously in the nation's woods. Our parks are poor mean things compared to King Christian's urban woods. Any man of an imaginative turn might seek and discover spiritual inspiration in such beauteous nooks as these. Their stillness too is so impressive and soothing. If Hyde Park were a wood instead of a pond, some grass, trees here and there, and so many flower-beds, Londoners would not be forced to complain of nerves quite so much.

The serried masses of the tree trunks would shut off the wearisome hum and buzz of metropolitan life, and a man might then draw a deep breath of comfort and peace right in the bowels of the town.

Save the café waiter—a gnome of a man—the only person I found in this enchanting plantation was a young lady with a novel. She could have had no better setting for her fiction—the pale blue Cattegat glimmering through the trees, the laced green branches above her, a gentle twitter of bird song, and not an obtrusive male within a mile of her. She did but glance at me, and then drew the garments of her romance again about her soul.

Dinner at the hotel Royal was a wonderful meal for the money, and the company was very genteel. I was reminded by a neighbour that this is the second hotel in Denmark, that of the Angleterre, in Copenhagen, being the first. There is, however, no magnificence here in Aarhus. Even the coffee-room is just an ordinary double apartment, with a bar in one division, and red velvet chairs and seats to little tables, with newspapers (not one English) thrown about. But it is dignified by the prospect of the great square outside, by the well-mannered waiters, and the company. Some of the elderly merchants of Aarhus, who came hither for their morning coffee and afternoon and evening gossip, were very entertaining figure-heads. Timber and dry goods, I was told, were accountable for their wealth—a fact that did not fire me with either enthusiasm or envy.

I waited for my "Sunbeam" by the afternoon train, and received it not. Nor did it come by the last train. Meanwhile, nothing remained but to get into choleric communication with Randers by telephone. The smith had, he said, nothing with which to reproach himself. The railway authorities, both at Randers and Aarhus, quite disclaimed responsibility. The cycle was no doubt on its journey. Why so much hurry? They managed the colloquy for me at the hotel. The final words were offered with a smile and a shoulder shrug.

"We do not do things so quick in Denmark," said the head-waiter, " but we do them."

I thought of smith Worsaae and shook my head. It seemed that I could be sure of nothing.

Then I went down to the sea for consolation and followed its coast-line, this time to the south, by new houses, and the common tokens of a town's extension. The headlands of Mols stood out from eight to sixteen miles away. If only they had been easily accessible, I would have gone to them at once. On Mols, it is said, you may find the thickest heads in all Denmark. The people cannot be called fools, because they know and admit the heritage. of stupidity bequeathed to them by their parents. It seemed to me that, in my present circumstances, I should find their obtuse skulls an eminent solace for my own lively irritation.

The coast south of Aarhus is after a mile or two a far-extending mass of woods, with low bluffs against the water's edge. The aspect of these woods is delightful, but they cannot be approached except from behind, where, a mile away, a road runs through a number of little sequestered villages—the home of the strawberries brought to the Aarhus market. I met groups of Aarhus families, with their hands full of flowers, returning from these sylvan retreats. And at Marselisborg, where there is a mill and a venerable mildewed and mossed *kro* and farm-house in one, there were scores of picnickers frolicking among the verdure. But the sight of their merriment did not, I am sorry to say, enliven me. I missed my companion grievously. There never was a better-natured friend than my poor "Sun-beam." Even when I loaded it with blame, most unjustly, it retaliated not, and at its best it served me right loyally.

Returning to the hotel at Aarhus, having by the way heard nothing encouraging from the crimson-collared station-master, I settled down to *dolce far niente* with the zeal of an established octogenarian. But I was not to be left in that easy situation. An agreeable middle-aged gentleman entangled me in conversation; we drank *bocks* together, and smoked cigars, and finally he haled me off to the Church of Our Lady, which, in his opinion, and mine, excels the cathedral in beauty. The same brick Gothic kind of building, which gives a certain squalor to a church. But its site is more in tune with the spirit of worship than that of the cathedral. It is in a sort of back-water from two or three busy streets, so that it faintly suggests in its environment the green calm of a cathedral close in our own dear land. Within there is much to charm in the graceful columns and groining and the well-chosen colours with which columns and vault are frescoed. Of old it was the chapel to an adjacent monastery of Dominicans. It is not now used, except as an appanage to the hospital which has succeeded the monks in the conventual buildings. Tombs of many kinds were here, and a very ornate little oratory. But the altar-piece held me most. It represented the Crucifixion in carved wood, freely coloured, and is the ablest group in Jutland. The dying thieves are, however, shown quite too appallingly agonized, and the scuffling at the foot of the crosses is more than a little barbarous.

At supper-time I was still without my cycle, and the next day was Sunday, when there is in Denmark but one delivery of goods.

Really it seemed as if I were destined to be an

annoyance in all the bettermost hotels of Jutland. But there was no help for it, and so I talked again, by telephone, with the railway people. In the answers that came back, one could almost see the outspread palms and heaves of the shoulders with which the officials emphasized their regrets. No accident had, however, happened on the line, and therefore, in time—

After supper I was carried by my acquaintance to Aarhus's one existing place of entertainment — a *café chantant*, though of the egregiously decorous kind.

"I often take my girls—the very little ones too. So you may see you shall not be shocked!" I was told earnestly.

The gardens in which the festive building stands were the best feature of the place. Still, even the entertainment was not despicable. But I did feel a little ashamed when a countryman of mine stepped on the stage and caricatured the British nation in the refined speech of Whitechapel. As a Hyde Park "exquisite," though himself anything but exquisite, he danced deplorable can-cans, and did other things; and the audience took it all seriously, and encored him all down the line.

"It is the English, my dear little child," I heard a sober old person inform his small pig-tailed daughter, who, though engaged with an ice cream, was clamorous to be instructed about the dancing man's meanings.

"Are they like that?" asked the child, reasonably astonished.

"Certainly they are. He is one himself," was the outrageous answer.

I was within an ace of disabusing the infant on this point, pricked on by patriotism. Who could tell what might not proceed from this tiny seed of lie thus sown in the child's mind? But I withheld myself. Perchance the man and his charge were natives of Mols. I took cowardly shelter behind this depraved aspiration.

There was, indeed, too much about England and the English in this Aarhus music-hall. A clever person sang "Ta-ra-ra-boom-de-ay" in every European language, to the various musical settings with which European composers have honoured the hideous canticle. The applause was immeasurable, and the whole hall resounded with the audience's echoings of the air. And a little later, when the clock was all but at closing time, a song was sung by a man in the guise of a pugilist, which I am afraid a good part of Aarhus believed to be a very important avowal of the secret of Anglo-Saxon eminence in the world. The gist of the first stanza was as follows: "Shall I tell you what gives British blood its strength on every shore? It is the lusty drink they imbibe which goes by the name of 'porter.' That is what invigorates John Bull throughout life's troubles. So

> Hurrah for hops, and hurrah for malt,
> For they are life's seasoning and salt."

I could not ascertain from my friend whether this song might be an advertisement of the London porter sold in his warehouse by one or other of the leading merchants of the town, by arrangement with the music-hall proprietor. But if I had heard the ingenuous child ask about the truth of the song, and its idiot of a father or grandfather answer that it was all truth, I really should have interfered with an informing word or two.

The concert ended with "Daisy Bell," "by special request," and this song carried the youth of Aarhus here assembled quite off their legs. The vocalist was not bad, I admit, but I had heard the song several times in England. We went out into the starlight, and left the hall in a tumult of gaiety.

And for an hour afterwards we sat with others outside our hotel, just as if it were France, smoking and listening to the cries for the waiter, and marking the unsteady movement of many of the passers-by. They don't mind sacrificing somewhat lavishly to thirst in Denmark on Saturday nights. Heaven knows, an Englishman can have no word to say in censure of such a practice outside his own country.

CHAPTER XVII

On Danish inns—Cathedral service—Aarhus excursionists—
An intelligent lad—Thorsager: its round church and
hospitable people—My heavy companion—Rönde—A
"forced" walk—The Lygten inn.

THE hotel Royal of Aarhus is the only Jutland inn
with walls to its bedrooms that do not bend to a
thump. At least, such is my experience. The chief
point about the average hostelry here is the fine
atmosphere of sociability that pervades it: if your
neighbour coughs in the night you sympathize profoundly with him; nor can he so much as turn in
his bed without the sound advising you of his
movements. But this sort of thing also has its
drawbacks. During my second night at Aarhus, I
was plagued by the disagreements of a husband
and wife in the next room. Even the brick walls did
not keep their little tiff from my ears. In any other
Jutland hotel the result would have been either
highly indelicate or something approximate to
maddening.

The best of July mornings opened with a rosy

dawn while my friends the other side of the wall paper were still bickering, and about five hours afterwards I rose and hearkened to the solemn tolling of the cathedral bell.

My first steps this day were rather profanely inspired. I did not go to church, like certain exemplary burghers and their wives, but with all speed to the railway station. Here they bandied me about from official to official, until I learnt my doom from a young man in the goods department. The cycle had not arrived. It was probably resting in peace on a by-line at Langaa. Nevertheless, I was not to be fretful. Without more than one doubt in ten, the particular van in which it reposed—with other articles marked " Immediate "—would be despatched to Aarhus in the course of the day, and I should have my property on the Monday. Unfortunately there was no chance of its arrival before the morrow. There must be some Spanish blood in Denmark, or else more of an Arctic congelation of energies than I had supposed.

However, I returned to the hotel, breakfasted on strawberries and cream, and bowed to the various gentlemen who bowed to me. The sky was adorably blue, and there was a pleasant breeze. I was able-bodied, and had the day before me. Certainly I ought not to have felt desperate.

Afterwards I went to church to listen to the

sermon. The great building was astonishingly supplied with congregation. There was no seat to spare,
and so I stood by a painted column and tried hard to
couple verbs and nouns together into the form of
such moral teaching as befitted my condition of soul.
The preacher was as strong in action as a Jesuit
missioner in Rome at Lent. His ruff quivered with
his quiverings and much aided his words. But the
blue sky was to be my sermon this day, and the larks
were to sing the anthem.

Perhaps, too, I should come in for a little more
human moralizing. My destination was Thorsager,
where there is a round church of wide fame. A
thousand years ago it was not a church, but a temple
of the northern kind, and hither the Jutlanders of
these parts came to do homage to the great god
Thor. No trace of the pagan worship remains except
the hill with the church now on it. According to
calculation, I seemed likely to reach Thorsager midway in the afternoon service.

There was real commotion at the small suburban
station whence I was to start. Such clean-faced
little boys and girls in their festival clothes, with
flowers (of which they were very conscious) in their
button-holes! They were clutched by terrified persons of the middle age and more, who did not seem
used to the trials of asking for a ticket. Like
alarmed sheep, these simple folks of Aarhus (if it

is possible to think they belonged to a town) swayed and surged before the cries and commands of the officials. Certain of the children wept bitterly, and few even of the oldsters were sufficiently experienced to spend these harassing moments of anticipation over discreet penny glasses of gin or cognac at the station bar.

Thorsager is about eighteen miles from Aarhus, and the line runs direct. I am thus explicit to prove that the extraordinary speed at which we travelled was really nothing out of the common. We were in fact two hours and ten minutes covering the distance. Yet the journey was not altogether dull. I was amused by my travelling companions, especially an old woman opposite me with a lemon-coloured face and spotless white lining and frill to her bonnet. I could have looked at her for weeks. She sat and breathed deeply, glancing from one to another of us, as if to judge how we also felt in this experimental feat of locomotion. It was a real loss when she had to leave us at Skjöldstrup. I held both her hands while she disembarked backwards, heedless of her ankles, she insisting that no other method of alighting suited her.

At all the little stations by the way—with peeps over the blue Cattegat in the east—the country groups were attractive. Every one seemed to be gripped by a mania for embracing. One pretty girl, with cheeks like the rose and corn-flower eyes, flew from face to face on the platform in a reckless manner. A small infantry soldier with a turned-up nose, and not even the mark of a corporal about him, was hugged by her accidentally. At least no other inference was to be made, for after the deed the others held up their hands as if shocked, the girl sobered immediately, and said something apparently apologetic to the warrior, and the warrior himself saluted in a very shy way, and moved rapidly towards another part of the platform. The Jutland male is not half a gallant individual.

I imagine our cargo consisted chiefly of servant-maids going home for the afternoon, and married people taking their children to be introduced to grandmamma and grandpapa, and to breathe the pure country air for a few hours. Well, it might have been worse. These scenes, by the way, were our redemption.

After Skjöldstrup I was left alone with a lively little boy of eleven or twelve and a meek-eyed widow who sat absurdly still with her hands folded in her lap. The boy had already pleased me. He behaved strangely for his years. For one thing, he smoked a pipe as if he were well used to it. For another, he had much to say to every damsel of his own time of life whose attention he could engage from the window. A well-dressed, pretty little fellow besides!

s

But he found me a problem, and when he had nothing else absorbing on hand he looked me over from boots to hat, with a frown of the most intense seriousness. The widow sat motionless, with downcast eyes.

Now just to show what Danish boys are capable of, I may as well tell what I did. This lad, at one time, having knocked his pipe empty with great noise, thrust his head from the window and engaged in amorous discourse with a girl he called Siegrid, in the next compartment, whose head was also presumably out of the window. His pipe lay empty on the seat. The idea took me to fill it from my own pouch, and then put it on the luggage rack out of his sight and reach. By and by he had had enough of Siegrid. He felt for his pipe, evidently surprised not to see it where he had left it; felt all his pockets, going redder and redder. Then he eyed the widow suspiciously. That foolish soul must needs smirk into a smile; whereupon the boy felt himself all over again, standing up, and then looked under the seat. His frowns were excellent. After which he said something impetuous and recurred to Siegrid, by and by sitting down again, to find the filled pipe where he had left it at first. But the silly widow had by this time buried her face in her handkerchief, as convulsed with laughter as a little while since perhaps she had been convulsed with sobs. You may imagine how red all this made the high-spirited lad. But he lit the pipe nevertheless and smoked it slowly, now and then looking into it as if to see what tobacco it was. The matter ended thus. When we neared Mörke the lad bustled about a bit, and when we stopped he took out a cigar-case, lifted his cap, and offered me a cigar with the words " *Vær saa god* " (Please !). He did it charmingly, so that I despaired of equalling him in courtesy. Afterwards, having left us, he rushed at Siegrid and pulled her ear so that she cried. And I lit the boy's cigar, and clouded the widow with his smoke. It was a very bad cigar, but I smoked it in his honour.

Several of us left the train at Thorsager. The village lies rather loftily, its church on a knoll in the middle of it. From the railway station the roundness of the latter was very observable ; its red hue was also surprising in this whitewashed land. About the base of its churchyard the thatched and tiled roofs of cottages with tall trees in their midst clustered prettily enough.

I was soon in the churchyard, having paused only to admire a confiding stork in a nest built on a broken house top. As I surmised, I had hit the time of service. The slumberous drone of the pastor's voice was audible when I was among the graves. It seemed best to tarry until the flock were

dismissed to their homes. And so I studied the
green and brown landscape to the north, with its
white dots which meant farmsteads; also the
church's exterior, and the two old runic stones
mounted in its red-brick walls. The building in its
nucleus is quite circular, but east, west, and south
bays proceed from it, the whole of trim old red
bricks, and the roofs leaded, with a conical leaded
stump tower from the middle part. Nothing could
look in better condition, and yet it is seven hundred
years since Bishop Vagnsen of Aarhus had its foundation stone laid.

While I rested on the north side of the churchyard the service ended and the villagers trooped
forth. The buzz of their voices drew me to the
porch. Here they were assembled, and clashing
tongues extraordinarily; all in black, with psalm-
books in their hands, which seemed to aid them in
gesticulating. The women's faces were the more ex-
pressive: their brownness and well-marked wrinkles
told of the field labour the hay season had forced
upon them. The men, self-indulgent wretches, were
hard at work stuffing their long pipes preparatory
to the stroll homewards. But both pipe-filling and
the chatter ceased when I appeared. All Thorsager
asked with its eyes who the stranger was. A churchwarden or deacon was instructing the people on
some point from within the porch as they passed

him by. His words now fell so flat that he wasted no more of them on deaf ears, but moved into the middle of the church instead. Thither I followed him, smiled on by a kindly woman who had first trodden hard on my toes.

The church is the scantiest and quaintest in Jutland. Its four brick columns supporting the central dome somewhat obstruct a general view of it and crowd it, but the effect pleases nevertheless. All is red-brick—the floor, the walls and the columns. The bright frescoes here and there by no means interfere with the harmony of the whole. I almost expected a red-brick pastor, but when the gentleman came courteously towards me from his vestry, with the words "Welcome to Denmark!" on his lips, he was seen to differ no way from his other brethren of the pulpit. True, I was unprepared for so warm a greeting. But I learned later that I owed it to the visit some few years ago of an English professor who somewhat resembled me, and who had made the Thorsager pulses flutter by his hot praises of the round church.

The pastor at once placed himself at my disposal as a guide. But he had little to tell me except that his church was round and "very old," and that he greatly admired the altar oil-painting by Herr Dorph. This latter seemed to me a poor thing, and of course it lacked the mellowness of its surroundings. Otherwise, there is nothing here, unless you set the imagination overturning the Christian church, and re-establishing the grove of the pagans.

Thorsager declined to let me go my way without a taste of its hospitality. I was given by the pastor into the hands of his churchwarden or deacon, who led me into a garden and house about three steps from the churchyard. First, we sat in the open, under a spreading elm tree. Then ladies began to appear, and we received them in the gentleman's parlour. I was urged to smoke, but between almost every pair of whiffs I had to rise and shake hands, and acknowledge the kindly " *Velkommen!* " of a fresh young lady, or one not quite young. The parlour was soon full of them, and a door was opened into another room for the overflow. Then mankind clumped in, with radiant neckties and a bashfulness that its victims resented. The situation threatened even worse things, for I had to make nearly all the conversation, and the early comers could not but detect my painful barrenness and lack of originality in ideas. I am sorry to say too they were not a very prepossessing company.

Eventually we drank coffee and ate biscuits, and I shook all their hands heartily and departed for Rönde. But I was not alone. They had pressed upon me for companion the most lumpish young man of them all, with a necktie visible at a distance of perhaps five miles. Vain was it for me to declare I could find my way. I could not get out of the lad, and so together we climbed the hill between the poppied barley fields, among which the storm in the night on Saturday had not acted benignly. But I understood when we were the other side of the little watershed, quite out of sight of Thorsager. For there, sitting on the turf, beneath a hawthorn, were two resplendent damsels who had not been to church (I should else have noticed their colours when they departed) and who rose to their feet when we appeared. My comrade's mouth broadened and broadened as we drew nearer. Then, when it seemed inevitably about to smile as never mouth yet had smiled, it opened.

"I do not go any farther," it said.

I left the young gentleman in this enviable plight. The damsels had him by the arms and were caressing his ears with their tender confidences. They looked as if they could eat him between them. But I am positive they would have found him tough.

The blue Cattegat and wooded Mols before me now, while for two miles I followed plain field paths towards the houses of Rönde on a slope to the left, were just the company I most desired. This was the Jutland I had learnt to love: innocent and green inland as a new-shelled pea, with the ever-faithful larks choiring overhead.

I hurried along to Rönde when I reached the high-road—such a thoroughfare as my "Sunbeam" would have rejoiced in. Also, having come to the Rönde *kro*, quite an assuming edifice of two storeys, with balconies, I begged them to give me supper with the utmost speed. I wished afterwards to run to the coast of the Bay of Kalö, so gracefully shut in with hills on the east, where stands a castle ruin whose walls once held Gustavus Vasa a prisoner of State. But from this enterprise I was dissuaded. I was told that two hours' hard walking would barely bring me to Lygten, whence I was to return to Aarhus by train, and that an hour and a half was necessary to take me to the castle and back.

The supper at Rönde was simple yet excellent: a spring chicken, and strawberries and cream. Afterwards, when I paid my reckoning, the maid formally presented me with a cigar on behalf of her mistress. "For luck!" she said. Though not of the best quality, it was yet better than the boy's in the train; and, like this other, it was none the less good for the way in which I came by it.

Then, quite late in the evening, I took to the road for my eight-mile walk. There were trees by the wayside, and the level was most agreeable. The views of Kalö Bay, with not a sail on it, soothed the mind. These views were best by Rolskov, whence I looked from a fair elevation across a broken green country, with a forested headland in the foreground. Again I yearned for my "Sunbeam." Several heated cyclists passed me on the road at a ridiculous pace, unless they were running for a wager. Such a district merited leisurely enjoyment. Every farmstead in its hollow or on its green hillock, with kine thickly in its glorious meadows, was a winsome picture of the rural life. And the weakening sunlight on the water, and on the paling purple hills of Mols, wrought pictorial wonders that it were a crime not to acknowledge with steady notice and admiration.

But even I need not have hurried as I did. At the *kro* of Lygten they gave me three-quarters of an hour ere the train might arrive.

There were two cyclists drinking beer at this inn, one of whom had a few words of ill-conditioned English. He had drunk quite enough beer, or else he would not have brought his nation into disesteem by the constant iteration of his English phrases, which were rather exclamatory (and impolite) than an aid to conversation. The youth dogged me even on the platform, as if he could not bear to keep his learning under a bushel. Every one like me waiting for the train wondered at him, and especially a young lady on the arm of a noncommissioned officer. But eventually his friend yielded to persuasion, and carried him off to put him to bed.

They were a tired, flower-laden troop of excursionists who travelled back by this train into the midst of the anxieties of metropolitan life in Aarhus.

CHAPTER XVIII

From Aarhus to Veile—Woods and valleys by Veile—Jellinge
and its royal tombs—The Jellinge runic stones—By the
Veile Fiord—Lone ladies under the beech trees.

THE end was at hand. Informed by the hotel
chambermaid early the next day that my "Sunbeam" had come, having travelled from the station
ignominiously recumbent on the roof of the omnibus,
I sped down-stairs to view it. And its condition was
what I had feared yet again. For all the tinkering
it had received, it still trailed a wounded hind wheel;
nor could I do aught to heal it. I had had enough
and more than enough of the Jutland smiths, and
the idea of interviewing one more of them in Aarhus
did not so much as enter my head.

It was a wet morning besides. I could hardly see
the cathedral vane through the thick air, and the
market-place was deserted and sloppy. And so we
lifted anchor and departed from Jutland's metropolis by the first train for the south.

All the way to Veile it continued to rain.
Scanderborg and its lakes had a sodden look. The

people by the way and travelling with me seemed resigned to storm weather. With the wind south-west, and a falling barometer, that was only too probable. But I had already telegraphed for a berth on the home-going steamer from Esbjerg the next afternoon. A stolid indifference had got hold of me, and I cared nothing for the swollen puddles in the highways visible from the train.

Still, in a more favourable season, these East Jutland roads would have been most tempting, with their avenues of trees, good construction, and real picturesqueness in a quiet way.

At Veile hope shone in the blue between the rain-clouds. Here I left my poor "Sunbeam" with the station-master and made arrangements for the night. Also I dined, with the usual company of German traders, whose sample cases cumbered the corridors, the sky brightening fast between the soup and the cheese. The strawberries and cream were no less praiseworthy here than farther north.

Afterwards, once more a pedestrian, I borrowed a stick and went in search of the biggest viking pimples in all Jutland, the tombs of King Gorm and his Queen Thyra, who were laid under the grass nearly a thousand years ago.

I should not have cared to make the excursion on my "Sunbeam." This is a district of hills, with deep valleys. The first climb from the town to the top of a wooded ridge was quite severe, and all the seven or eight miles to Jellinge, where the dead king and his wife are buried, were ascents and descents almost as abrupt. The scenery amazed me by its beauty. Just outside the town the views over the Veile Fiord were of high quality, with much wood as well as water to be seen, and red houses dotting the green hill-sides and meadows.

One beech wood about half-way to Jellinge was particularly pleasant. It hung to the steep sides of a declivity which the road traversed, and was full of black shadow among the tree trunks. Not a bird piped from this sombre forest. I had not seen a soul for a mile. But from the darkness at my side there crept forth such a bowed old woman, with a hooked nose and eager eyes under heavy brows, that I might have been excused for fancying her a witch, or a survival of the times of King Gorm. The poor creature had been pilfering sticks in defiance of the notice-boards, however, and was much more terrified of me than a witch would have been. She had no intelligible speech for me save a "Thank you" when I paid deference to her poverty and decrepitude.

A turn of the road, and there was an end to the spirit of eerie gloom which sat on every twig of this beech wood. A green valley was below, with meadows and a river. Right in its midst a red mill was set, with extensive outbuildings and cattle scattered among the grass land. And the throbbing of its wheel filled the valley with murmurous sound, which the dense trees on the slopes all up the valley on both sides kept from dissipating itself unduly. The mill and other red houses peeping from the verdure argued a village, and so did the group of boys and girls whom I met by the mill bridge, with school-books in their hands, wooden clogs to their feet, and much chatter and laughing on their tongues.

Two miles or so from Jellinge the road kept determinedly uphill. The old landscape of heathery ridges reappeared, with the old decoration of little rounded swellings. It was to be expected. A district that was good enough for the interment of the king and queen of all Denmark was likely to attract his loyal thanes in need of graves. After Gorm and Thyra the monarchs of the land, whether Pagan or Christian at heart, were under some constraint to lie in the churches that had begun to decorate Denmark's woods with their granite walls. But, as a mere matter of sentiment, perhaps the vikings under turf mounds, with bell-heather and blue-bells flowering over them, had pleasanter graves than those whom the new civilization and faith put under church paving-stones.

Jellinge is a unique village. A thousand years ago it was nothing but a couple of very large pimples on the upland, divided by a space of fifty or seventy yards; and a couple of runic stones, the one set up by King Gorm to commemorate his dead queen, the other devised by King Harold Bluetooth in honour of his parents, King Gorm and Queen Thyra. Christianity, however, made haste to erect a church midway between the pimples, and the runic stones are now in the churchyard. Later, the Danes of long ago found the vicinity of their dead pagan monarchs and that of the church very congenial for residential purposes. And now red and white houses press the tombs and the church on all sides, and the sober course of Jutland village life proceeds here quite unaffected by King Gorm and Queen Thyra, whose mounds lift their green tops just above the highest of the houses, though they in their turn have to yield pre-eminence by a few feet to the white belfry of the old church. The moderns have planted a flagstaff over Queen Thyra. It rattles a good deal in the wind, but does no particular harm. A granite slab has also been let into the mound on one side, with initials and the date 1873, to remind the visitor that King Christian the Ninth once came hither and gave his notable ancestors the tribute of a thought or two.

Having a church, an inn, a railway station, and a school, Jellinge is of course well fitted now-a-days to scorn the pagans, who heaped all this earth in the middle of the village. But it rather enjoys its distinction. It has scratched paths on the pimples, and its photographer has in his *atelier* (he calls it that) photographs of the mounds and the runic stones. The school-children, however, most of all find their pleasure over the dead monarch and his spouse. The sides of the mounds are apt to become divinely slippery; and you may see the youngsters, as I saw them, going in procession from the top to the bottom, like sliders on ice, with much shouting. This was the more marked on Queen Thyra's mound. In the queen's day she was called "*Danebod*," or the "Danes' joy." She is singularly blessed to be still the occasion of considerable joy nearly a thousand years after they enclosed her in the oak chamber in the heart of the pimple. It is to be hoped she was, as some say, an English woman. She deserves to be borne in mind for the great wall or "work" near Schleswig, by which it was proposed to keep the marauding Germans of the south for ever aloof from Denmark.

Queen Thyra's tomb is the only one of its kind in Jutland adapted for visitation. There is a wooden door in its side, and through this you may go into the timbered apartment under the sods wherein she lay. Of course nothing of interest has been left in the tomb. In 1861 the trifles left by previous ransackers were finally removed to Copenhagen, where they may be seen in that most interesting of all national museums. So little does Jellinge think her Majesty's last resting-place worth exploiting as a source of revenue, that no one in the village of whom I inquired knew who kept the key of the door. The general opinion indeed was that there was no key, although there was a conspicuous keyhole. But it did not perhaps matter very much.

On the other hand, King Harold Bluetooth's filial monument in the churchyard was there for all eyes to see, hard by the south porch, with the simple gravestones of the nineteenth-century dead close to it. It is a huge, wedge-shaped lump of granite, about nine feet high and broad, and four feet thick at the base: three-sided and sculptured on all three sides. The cross and the dragon appear in low relief on the stone, and a serpent coiled round the dragon. The lengthy inscription in runic character is as clear-cut as when the mason made his last scratch on the stone. I asked a young man with school-books in his hand, who was promenading past the stone, if he could enlighten me about the runic words. He had a scholarly face, and was evidently committing a lesson to heart. But my request baffled him.

"It is the same as this, for example," he said, pointing to a small white marble gravestone with "In Heaven!" written on it.

T

King Gorm's memorial to his queen is much less imposing than the other: some five feet high by three, and perhaps sixteen inches thick. But this also is closely sculptured with runes mysterious to the villagers who pass it on their way to church.

The view from the mounds was thoroughly Jutlandish, including many pimples or ridges, as well as a vast area of green country broken by little woods and white-faced villages. Happily the weather was no longer rough, and the blue cloud-flecked sky gave a certain grace even to the moor of Randbölhede, which begins a few miles south-west of the village.

I supped at the Jellinge *kro*, which promised ill at first sight. But there was a tolerable small *salon* as well as a very dirty common-room, and here they served me an excellent meal for thirteen-pence halfpenny.

The journey back to Veile by train disclosed some beautiful scenery, once we were down from the uplands. We got into the valleys between the beech woods, and moved very carefully among meadows crowded with ragged-robin and meadow-sweet, pervaded by the daintiest small trout streams, running briskly seawards, that ever an angler beheld. This railway is not, I believe, a State property. But its trains are as slow as any others in the land. On this lovely evening, however, the pace was of no consequence. We tarried briefly at several new little sheds in the valley, to which comely women with baskets of produce had come down from the woods to meet us. The remains of a factory or two, happily abandoned, made a startling show in this exquisite glen. On the fractured rim of the tall chimney of one of the buildings an enterprising stork had set up house. He and his youngsters were some eighty feet above the ground. They all thrust their red beaks forward to look at the train, so that there seemed some danger that the nest's equilibrium would be violently disturbed. But we steamed out of their orbit, and at length entered Veile, where we were discharged from a new branch station.

It was so heavenly an evening that I now strolled at a venture for the shore of the fiord. Whether I hit the north shore or the south shore, I cared little. The cool water-side air would serve equally well in either case.

The better part of Veile was abroad, it seemed, with the same intent. I crossed a high-road with so many people in it that the town at once trebled its population in my esteem : a pleasant high-road with trees to it and seats, and the promise of woods a little beyond. Then, by following certain young gentlemen and ladies, I came to the fiord side, and learnt why Veile is considered so beautiful.

The road ran into woods, with a dip on the right

to the water. Across the fiord were other woods, rising to a height of some three hundred feet. As far as could be seen up the fiord, perhaps six miles, its banks were all trees. An occasional villa gleamed through the woods, but neither village nor town. And the fiord between, a mile and more wide, was smooth and silvery, with five or six yachts trying to move without wind, and one tall schooner, well towards the sea, with all sails set for the westering sun to shine full upon. It was a lovely scene, thoroughly tranquil too in spite of the town at the head of the water-way, with its lofty church spire and two factory chimneys.

No town in Denmark can have more enchanting woods than Veile's. I walked fast for half-an-hour, hugging the fiord, and was then still under the shade of beeches and oaks, among toy bridges across pigmy ravines, and rustic seats above and beneath me; the water gradually taking the opaline tints of which I had seen so much in Jutland, and the mid-summer air so still, though freshened by the fiord.

I should have supposed Veile's young men and maidens would, at such a time, have flown to this wood like bees to honey-flowers. But it was not so. There was a noisy drinking-house by the fiord, where the town quite ended, with a concert-room over the water. It was as if a local law forbade the Veile males to go past this house. Farther on I discovered lone ladies, sitting by twos and threes, whispering in the sylvan gloom, and met two companies of young damsels playing about like lambkins. But no man of any kind. It seemed to me that I was looked at with some suspicion. And yet I was unmistakably on a highway, with a railroad parallel and near, along which periodically a train moved shrieking as if it said, "For God's sake get out of my way! At the pace I am going I could not pull up until I had run ten yards after putting my brake on."

The fading daylight crept into the wood between the tree trunks from the west, and the sunset's gold stole upon the fiord. In about two miles I came to a fine house on a headland, with gardens and a band-stand. This was one of Veile's pleasure resorts. To-night, however, it was as good as empty. Per-haps five ladies were drinking coffee on its terrace. There were others in the remarkable rooms of evergreen stuff contrived on the slope of the head-land, with walls of box ten feet high, small tables inside, and romantic views from the fiord side, where the box was not planted. The dearth of my own sex was strangely oppressive.

To be sure, there were several swallow-tailed waiters, smoking and lolling on iron chairs. But they could not count. Methought too that, when called to provide more sugar or a spoon, they did their business without speaking, as if it were required of them.

And yet it was mere chance after all that left the Veile ladies without their most natural companions. The waiter whom I asked about the mystery, said that usually there were plenty of gentlemen in the gardens.   Perhaps the programme at the *café chantant* nearer the town was a peculiarly strong one. But even then it said little for the taste of the Veile youth.

From these gardens by the water-side the sun set majestically behind Veile's roofs, the spire, and the two chimney stacks. The schooner stayed where it had been, and closed the fiord so that it seemed a lake. And the yachts still vainly pleaded for a puff of wind. But the woods darkened ominously, so that not even the gold and crimson and turquoise of the sky above could give them back their earlier charm.

Returning under the beech trees in the twilight, the sombre shapes of women were discernible amid the trunks, sitting and thinking, with their faces turned towards the fiord. But still no men.

At the *café chantant*, however, there was a riot of clinking glasses and song, and a cry of " *Bis!* " taken up by fifty voices.

CHAPTER XIX

A wet last day in Jutland—Fredericia and the Little Belt—
Where the Danes fought well—Kolding—Kolding Castle—
One more stork—More storm weather—The Swede and
the Dane—Esbjerg—A rough night.

IT was certainly well that we had done with
Jutland for the present. In spite of the flaunting
glory of the sunset, the next morning at Veile
opened dismally, with wet streets, flying rain-clouds,
and the inn courtyard visible from my window
beset with cocks and hens, whose plumage bore
witness to the energy of the recent showers.

And yet, leaving Veile for the south by the first
train, I was, ere fifteen minutes had passed, half
inclined to call "Halt!" and upbraid myself for my
cowardice. The train carried us—oh, so carefully!—
through the woods high up on the fiord's southern
shore. We got glimpses of the squall-swept water
below, but these were nothing compared to the
charm of the woods themselves. Between the
masses of oaks, beeches, and pines, now and again
trim meadows showed, with a red house as trim as

279

the meadows and kine with generous udders cropping buttercups by the house. The scenery was at its best by Munkebjerg, where there is a hotel, and whither the Veile folk come by water as well as train for picnic purposes.

But resignation soon set in again. The old tameness of the Jutland landscapes reappeared, and the weather worsened. My fellow-travellers, who had become riotously talkative in the wood, lapsed into silence, and puffed at their pipes with faces like the faces of stone images.

In an hour we were at Fredericia, with some dubious sunshine over us, and the Little Belt making a baby fuss with its baby waves.

Fredericia is rather an agreeable little town, famous for its fresh air. The great island of Fyen is only a mile away, with heavy ferry-boats plying between it and Jutland. A fair sprinkling of forest trees on its shores makes this island seem from Fredericia far more picturesque than it is. Inland it is one vast plain, exceedingly fertile but distinctly unbeautiful. Fredericia has bright *boulevards* along its coast-line, but they do not go far, and when you get past the fortifications to the north and out of the borough to the south, you must find what pleasure you can in a scramble along the Jutland shore with no road in particular to aid you.

Very different was my last sojourn in this little

town, of which Denmark is so proud for its victory
in July 1849 over the German invaders. Then
the Belt was all but fast. The weighty iron ferry-
boat could just crush its way through the mile-long
channel of broken congealing floes. On either hand
the Belt was ice, the red January sun illumining
bravely the sea-green and blue edges of the up-
turned, welded blocks. Sportsmen after duck could
be seen stealing from one ice-shelter to another, with
fitful cracking of their guns. And I too, late in the
evening, under a gay full moon, put on skates and
adventured north-east into the open sea. This was,
I learned afterwards, not quite the thing a wise man
would have done; they told me that night at the
inn of a certain excellent baker of the town who
had thus disappeared only the previous week. But
I enjoyed a rough biting hour or two, and did not
disappear like the baker. And the next day, having
paid homage to the grave of the five hundred Danes
who fell fighting for their fatherland, I proceeded
east, and came near spending a day and a night
frozen up in the Great Belt, the crossing of which
was almost an adventure. This was in the winter
of 1892. Denmark expects rarely to be treated by
King Frost with such severity.

We were of course kept waiting at Fredericia on
this July day. The Copenhagen train was late. An
hour passed, and still we did not move on to

Kolding. But there was the usual entertainment in admiring the exteriors of the railway officials, and contrasting the pipe-bowl of one phlegmatic Jutlander with the pipe-bowl of his neighbour. Further, I read the telegraphic notice of the weather in various parts of the realm, and was interested to learn that Esbjerg's message was, " Clouded, high winds from the south-west, and rain." In response to which I could but hope that King Christian was by that evening's boat to England sending us plenty of bacon and butter to steady the ship, and that the crush of travellers would not be unusual.

As for my " Sunbeam," it might as well now be crippled as not. I no longer pined to be upon it, nor did I give it much thought.

At last we ambled on to Kolding. In all I was three hours reaching that engaging seaport, the distance by road from Veile being about fifteen miles. Not even a succession of feasts on strawberries and cream and comparatively trivial hotel bills can quite reconcile the Briton on tour to such dreadfully slow sauntering through life. On one's own legs it might be otherwise. But when payment is made to be moved by steam, one does expect a rate of locomotion above that of which any common coach hack would be ashamed.

Kolding is remarkable for one of the most ugly

castle ruins in Christendom. I tarried to dine and
see the ruins. The dinner was well enough and
caused me some slight emotion as I ate my last
strawberry in the land. But I was charged as much
for it here (on the direct route between Paris and
the northern capitals) as I had paid for a day's
board and lodging in Jutland's unsophisticated
wilds. The view from the hotel coffee-room of a
certain gabled building across the square somewhat
atoned for the extortion. It was a red-brick house
intersected with timbers, the extremities fantastic-
ally carved, the best relic of mediæval domestic
architecture I had seen in Jutland; and over its
porch I read later, in old German, the text, "Except
the Lord build the house, etc." The house is now-a-
days a shop, and the proprietor hastened out to me
while I was occupied with his inscription. "With
what could he supply me?" he begged to know. I
bought nothing from him, but elsewhere in the town
I bought a pound of tobacco for fifteen-pence; such
tobacco too as a gentleman might smoke in his
bedroom without fear of suffocating the chambermaid the next morning.

But the castle was the thing. Strange to say,
though such an enormous pile, it took some finding.
I wandered well out into the country seeking it, and
yet it lies close at the back of the hotel. But the
walk was not wasted. It showed me some pretty

old almshouses, with a saintly appellation which
I forget, and having a conspicuous board on which
the names of certain vegetables were written.
The honoured public were entreated to purchase
these superfluous roots from the almshouse garden
for the good of the funds of the charity. Here or
hereabouts too I looked on my last stork. The dear
bird was on one leg, and held his right cheek nursed
in the broad of his other foot. At least this was the
impression his attitude created. Some jackdaws
croaked over him, but did not disturb him. He was
without wife or children, and stood alone in an untidy
nest, such as you would expect a bachelor's to be.
I would have given a crown to the almshouse fund
to know if the poor bird had toothache, or if he was
reflecting dismally, like some of the rest of us, about
his mistake in not seeking a wife in the heyday of
his strength and beauty. The lady would at least
have known how to compose the sticks of his home
so that their ends did not tickle him into irascibility
every time he lay down in them. And of what use,
pray, to be ill-natured and angry when there is no
Mrs. Stork to vent one's feelings upon? The poor
bird's tail feathers lifted unbecomingly in the breeze,
which also swayed him as he stood thus balanced.
Never was there such a picture of woeful inde-
pendence. But no young lady stork was moved to
compassion for him. He was still unsolaced when I

left him in the agonies of toothache or heartache. His nearest attendant was a chimney-pot, which dribbled smoke at him.

I cannot better describe Kolding's castle in the rough than by mentioning a Stockport cotton-mill. Take a very large mill, and rear a tower at one end of it, with windows much like those of the body of the building, and you have Kolding Castle. Only you must dismantle the block—remove its roof and knock out all its glass and partition walls. Then, if you perch the edifice on a small hill, with trees sloping down to a good-sized pond, for the ruin to reflect itself in, and put a few architectural odds and ends in the chambers opening from the main hall of the ruin, you have Kolding Castle to the life, or rather the death.

It is almost inconceivable how any king could have chosen such a castle for his habitation; or, having had it erected, should not straightway have given orders for its demolition.

Nevertheless, this castle cannot be despised. Its hugeness evokes a certain feeling of respect, and no doubt they are right who say that when the moon is up the place is even beautiful. As a site for storks' nests, it is perhaps unmatched in Denmark. Yet no stork abides on its red-brick heights. These are left to the jackdaws, who have much to tell each other a couple of hundred feet above the head of the visitor to the ruins.

" There is," I learned from a notice-board, " admission to the *slot* gardens for all well-clothed persons." Our Danish cousins are not often so pointedly hard on poverty. But the restriction is at least eloquent testimony to the general well-being of the provincial Dane. We in England could not afford to be so particular. Westminster Abbey is as free to the barefooted vagabond as to the American millionaire.

The lady who, for threepence, conducted me into the castle shell, soon exhausted her descriptive powers. Some of the stonework to the window-frames and portals merits a compliment, and I was expected to ejaculate when I was brought under the great tower and could look up at its lofty summit. There was little else to impress, though an artist was here frowning hard at his canvas, which was as truthful as the average critic would require it to be.

The *slot's* garden is better than the *slot*. Having parted from my guide, who had the common desire to sell a few photographs, I sat on a bench among the elder bushes, and looked at the swans on the pond. I looked also right away to the north, across the little red houses of the suburbs, at the wild moorlands of Jutland that I had now done with. Not one viking pimple was to be seen. And yet a single one of these familiar suggestive mounds, with their heathery beards, would have given Kolding's castle a hold on my heart.

Traces of the ancient times when the king lived here were abundant outside the principal entrance to the castle. Some acres of palatial stabling, with a spacious courtyard in their midst, were to be seen. All apparently disused now; not even applied to other purposes. These empty stalls gave a better idea of the castle's greatness once upon a time than its own red-brick walls.

There is a respectable church in Kolding as well as a castle. It looks new, but is not. Its red bricks are strangely red, and its spire tries to get as near the clouds as the castle tower. Inside, however, one perceives from its mortuary tablets, which abound, that it has enjoyed a long lease of life already. The altar has a singular painting of Christ holding His heart in His hand, and of a woman seated at an easel, with colour box, brushes, etc., making a copy of Christ's heart: "*Imitatione Christi.*" In truth, the church is most memorable for the fine show pigments make in it. Nearly all the sixteenth-century portrait tablets have been freshly coloured. The pulpit of 1591 dazzles with its painted woodwork, and the font bears a *baldacchino* that is nothing less than startling in its pyramidal arrangement of faces, heads, and nude busts, brighter than reality, and tricked out with an exuberance of decorative flourishes, upon which the artist has smeared colours with extraordinary effect. As a rule, the Jutland church worships whitewash and that alone, but having decided that other touches are admissible, it then goes in recklessly for the whole paint-box. Many of these Kolding mural tablets have the inscription, "God give him a happy resurrection." One may apply the same wish to the church itself in its decorative details; though many years will have to elapse before the pulpit, organ case, font, and other garish objects can lose their rainbow-like effulgence. After all, the old pagans had the best of it in choosing woods for their cathedrals. But civilization has many mouths to fill, and cannot afford to dispense with architects and builders, down to the makers of spittoons for the church aisles and the pastor's pulpit.

With rain again falling and a tempestuous wind, it was time to leave Kolding for Esbjerg. Every mile of the road helped us towards worse weather. At Lunderskov, where we parted from the bulk of the train, bound pleasantly for Hamburg, the storm shook the carriages; and at Bramminge, the last junction, there was no keeping either wind or rain out of our midst. Only three of us stayed on to Bramminge, which is as much as to say Esbjerg, which, in its turn, almost implies England. Of the other two, one was a large Swede, in blue serge, who smiled at the storm, and the second was a smart young Dane, who appeared to be bent on seeking his fortune in America. Both men agreed that Scandinavia was a poor part of the world for a person with ambition and ability.

"I," said the Swede, "do not care how much it blows on the sea. I go to my bed and I sleep, and when I am in England I am with my brother, who has a large mill. I need not exert myself when I am with my brother."

The young Dane, on the other hand, did not, he confessed, know a soul out of Denmark.

"But in America there is work for all; is it not so?" he inquired.

I expressed my opinion, and he smoked the more cheerfully for my answer.

The Swede looked at the Dane rather contemptuously after this and remarked that he would not care to be in his shoes.

"It is not easy being alone in the world like that," he said.

I expect, however, the young Dane will have the better of the deal. By the way he controlled himself, instead of retorting that every man has not a brother with a large mill to sponge on, he proved himself a lad of mettle and prudence. Also, he meant to travel second-class to Harwich, he said, although his watch-chain was of superior gold to that of the Swede, who hoped to have a cabin to himself.

The rain affected the movements of a blizzard when we turned out on the quay close to the *Koldinghus,* whose crane was busy upon a stupendous heap of butter boxes. The few passengers for the voyage had nestled in the saloon and the smoking-room.

It behoved me, however, to get off to the hotel when I had seen my blemished "Sunbeam" tied fast in the hold. There I found the fat boy-waiter, smiling upon my bag and coat, which he had not, in spite of a telegram, sent on board the steamer.

"I shall accompany you with them at once," he said ; but I dissuaded him.

We made a heavy start about seven o'clock in the evening, and were soon being shaken lustily. Three Swedish ladies were among the company : two young, and one a little more than young. They were treating themselves to a tour in Scotland, knowing no English. One of them asked me if the expense of hotel life in the Trossachs and the Highlands differed much from that in Denmark. I sincerely hope their pleasure has not been spoiled by the realization of the truth in this matter.

Fanö's yellow sands looked the yellower for the black, howling clouds over them. When we lost them we lost Jutland. But we did not lose them until we had been at sea about three hours. Our good captain, having ascertained that his compass was defective, employed seventy or eighty minutes in going round on the same area of turbulent waters.

We used as a centre for this purpose a certain fishing-boat, whose crew must at times have thought our skipper a madman. Once indeed they hailed him with sounding words. This was on the fifth occasion, when he brought the *Koldinghus* within a stone's throw of the smack's bows.

But we got away at last, and six-and-thirty hours later the mountainous coast of Suffolk was near at hand. After Jutland, even our eastern counties seemed strangely elevated.

THE END

RICHARD CLAY & SONS, LIMITED
LONDON & BUNGAY.

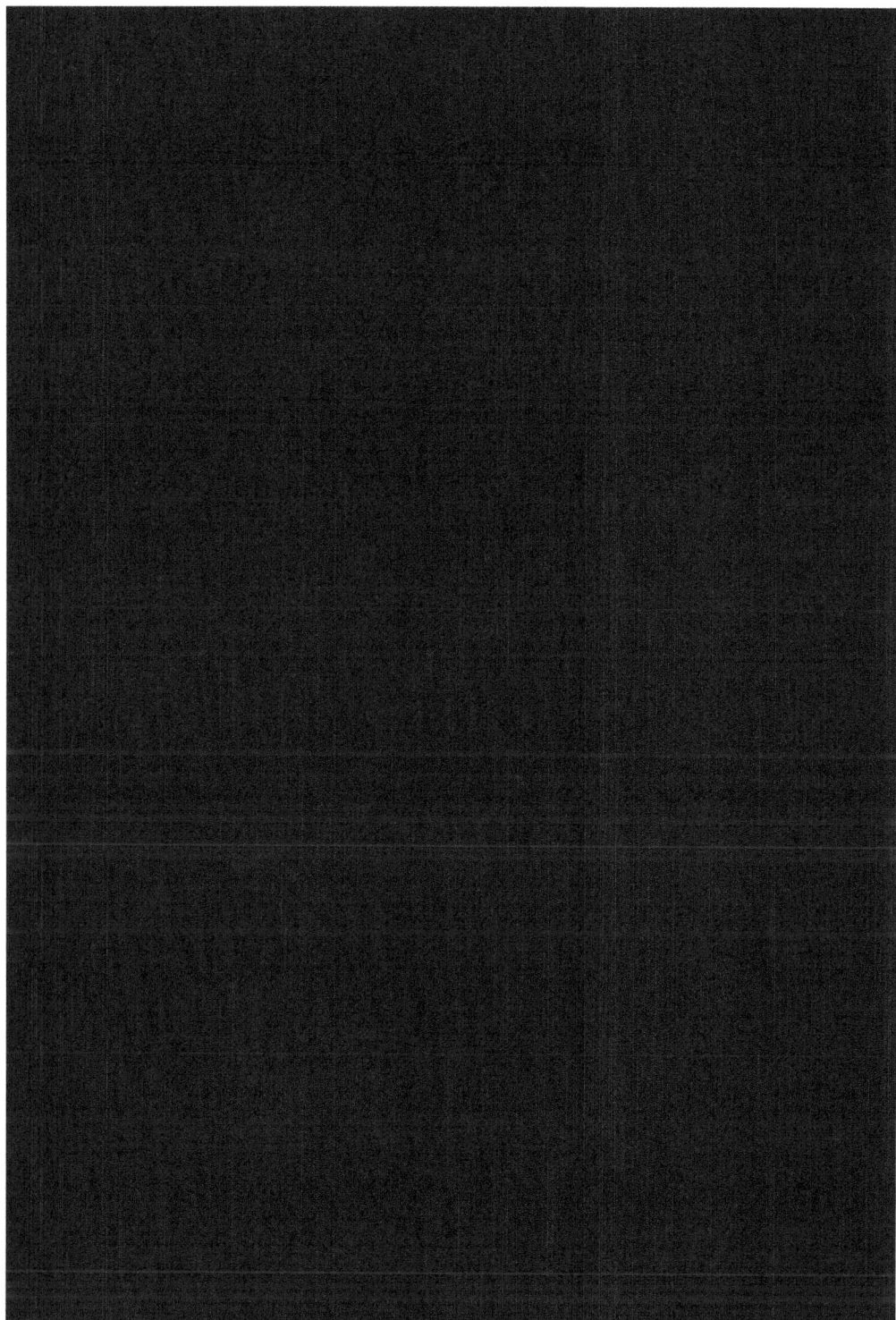

CPSIA information can be obtained at www.ICGtesting.com
Printed in the USA
BVOW09s1216170715

409284BV00018B/237/P